Switched Networks Lab Manual

Cisco Networking Academy

Cisco Press
800 East 96th Street
Indianapolis, Indiana 46240

Switched Networks Lab Manual

Cisco Networking Academy

Copyright © 2014 Cisco Systems, Inc.

Published by:
Cisco Press
800 East 96th Street
Indianapolis, IN 46240 USA

Printed in the United States of America

First Printing December 2013

ISBN-13: 9781587133275

ISBN-10: 158713327X

Warning and Disclaimer

This book is designed to provide information about Switched Networks. Every effort has been made to make this book as complete and as accurate as possible, but no warranty or fitness is implied.

The information is provided on an "as is" basis. The authors, Cisco Press, and Cisco Systems, Inc. shall have neither liability nor responsibility to any person or entity with respect to any loss or damages arising from the information contained in this book or from the use of the discs or programs that may accompany it.

The opinions expressed in this book belong to the author and are not necessarily those of Cisco Systems, Inc.

Trademark Acknowledgments

All terms mentioned in this book that are known to be trademarks or service marks have been appropriately capitalized. Cisco Press or Cisco Systems, Inc., cannot attest to the accuracy of this information. Use of a term in this book should not be regarded as affecting the validity of any trademark or service mark.

This book is part of the Cisco Networking Academy® series from Cisco Press. The products in this series support and complement the Cisco Networking Academy curriculum. If you are using this book outside the Networking Academy, then you are not preparing with a Cisco trained and authorized Networking Academy provider.

For more information on the Cisco Networking Academy or to locate a Networking Academy, please visit www.cisco.com/edu.

CISCO.

Feedback Information

At Cisco Press, our goal is to create in-depth technical books of the highest quality and value. Each book is crafted with care and precision, undergoing rigorous development that involves the unique expertise of members from the professional technical community.

Readers' feedback is a natural continuation of this process. If you have any comments regarding how we could improve the quality of this book, or otherwise alter it to better suit your needs, you can contact us through email at feedback@ciscopress.com. Please make sure to include the book title and ISBN in your message.

We greatly appreciate your assistance.

Publisher	**Paul Boger**
Associate Publisher	**Dave Dusthimer**
Business Operations Manager, Cisco Press	**Jan Cornelssen**
Executive Editor	**Mary Beth Ray**
Managing Editor	**Sandra Schroeder**
Project Editor	**Seth Kerney**
Editorial Assistant	**Vanessa Evans**
Cover Designer	**Mark Shirar**
Compositor	**TnT Design, Inc.**

Americas Headquarters	Asia Pacific Headquarters	Europe Headquarters
Cisco Systems, Inc.	Cisco Systems (USA) Pte. Ltd.	Cisco Systems International BV
San Jose, CA	Singapore	Amsterdam, The Netherlands

Cisco has more than 200 offices worldwide. Addresses, phone numbers, and fax numbers are listed on the Cisco Website at **www.cisco.com/go/offices.**

CCDE, CCENT, Cisco Eos, Cisco HealthPresence, the Cisco logo, Cisco Lumin, Cisco Nexus, Cisco StadiumVision, Cisco TelePresence, Cisco WebEx, DCE, and Welcome to the Human Network are trademarks; Changing the Way We Work, Live, Play, and Learn and Cisco Store are service marks; and Access Registrar, Aironet, AsyncOS, Bringing the Meeting To You, Catalyst, CCDA, CCDP, CCIE, CCIP, CCNA, CCNP, CCSP, CCVP, Cisco, the Cisco Certified Internetwork Expert logo, Cisco IOS, Cisco Press, Cisco Systems, Cisco Systems Capital, the Cisco Systems logo, Cisco Unity, Collaboration Without Limitation, EtherFast, EtherSwitch, Event Center, Fast Step, Follow Me Browsing, FormShare, GigaDrive, HomeLink, Internet Quotient, IOS, iPhone, iQuick Study, IronPort, the IronPort logo, LightStream, Linksys, MediaTone, MeetingPlace, MeetingPlace Chime Sound, MGX, Networkers, Networking Academy, Network Registrar, PCNow, PIX, PowerPanels, ProConnect, ScriptShare, SenderBase, SMARTnet, Spectrum Expert, StackWise, The Fastest Way to Increase Your Internet Quotient, TransPath, WebEx, and the WebEx logo are registered trademarks of Cisco Systems, Inc. and/or its affiliates in the United States and certain other countries.

All other trademarks mentioned in this document or website are the property of their respective owners. The use of the word partner does not imply a partnership relationship between Cisco and any other company. (0812R)

Contents

About This Lab Manual

Switched Networks Lab Manual contains all the labs and class activities from the Cisco Networking Academy course of the same name. It is meant to be used within this program of study.

More Practice

If you would like more practice activities, combine your Lab Manual with the new *CCNA Routing and Switching Practice and Study Guide* ISBN: 9781587133442

Other Related Titles

CCNA Routing and Switching Portable Command Guide ISBN: 9781587204302 (or eBook ISBN: 9780133381368)

Switched Networks Companion Guide ISBN: 9781587133299 (or eBook ISBN: 9780133476460)

Switched Networks Course Booklet ISBN: 9781587133268

Command Syntax Conventions

The conventions used to present command syntax in this book are the same conventions used in the IOS Command Reference. The Command Reference describes these conventions as follows:

- **Boldface** indicates commands and keywords that are entered literally as shown. In actual configuration examples and output (not general command syntax), boldface indicates commands that are manually input by the user (such as a **show** command).

- *Italic* indicates arguments for which you supply actual values.

- Vertical bars (|) separate alternative, mutually exclusive elements.

- Square brackets ([ ]) indicate an optional element.

- Braces ({ }) indicate a required choice.

- Braces within brackets ([{ }]) indicate a required choice within an optional element.

Chapter 1 — Introduction to Switched Networks

1.0.1.2 Class Activity – Sent or Received

Objectives

Describe convergence of data, voice, and video in the context of switched networks.

Scenario

Individually, or in groups (per the instructor's decision), discuss various ways hosts send and receive data, voice, and streaming video.

- Develop a matrix (table) listing network data types that can be sent and received. Provide five examples.

Your matrix table might look something like this:

Sent	Received
Client requests a web page from a web server.	Web server send web page to requesting client.

Save your work in either hard- or soft-copy format. Be prepared to discuss your matrix and statements in a class discussion.

Resources

Internet connectivity

Reflection

1. If you are receiving data, how do you think a switch assists in that process?

_____

2. If you are sending network data, how do you think a switch assists in that process?

_____

1.1.3.6 Lab – Selecting Switching Hardware

Objectives

Part 1: Explore Cisco Switch Products

Part 2: Select an Access Layer Switch

Part 3: Select a Distribution/Core Layer Switch

Background / Scenario

As a Network Engineer, you are part of a team that selects appropriate devices for your network. You need to consider the network requirements for the company as they migrate to a converged network. This converged network supports voice over IP (VoIP), video streaming, and expansion of the company to support a larger customer base.

For a small- to medium-sized company, Cisco hierarchical network design suggests only using a two-tier LAN design. This design consists of an access layer and a collapsed core/distribution layer. Network switches come in different form factors, and with various features and functions. When selecting a switch, the team must choose between fixed configuration or modular configuration, and stackable or non-stackable switches.

Based on a given set of requirements, you will identify the Cisco switch models and features to support the requirements. The scope of this lab will limit the switch models to campus LAN only.

Required Resources

PC with Internet access

Part 1:   Explore Cisco Switch Products

In Part 1, you will navigate the Cisco website and explore available switch products.

Step 1:   Navigate the Cisco website.

At www.cisco.com, a list of available products and information about these products is available.

a. From the home page, click **Products & Services** > **Switches**.

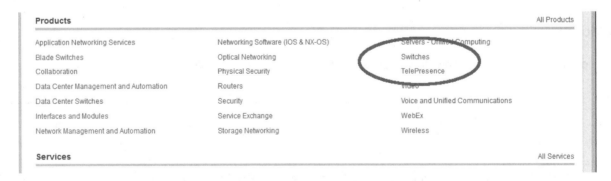

Step 2:   Explore switch products.

In the Feature Products section, a list of different categories of switches is displayed. In this lab, you will explore the campus LAN switches. You can click different links to gather information about the different switch models. On this page, the information is organized in different ways. You can view all available switches by clicking **View All Switches**. If you click **Compare Series**, the switches are organized by types: modular vs. fixed configuration.

Featured Products   View All Switches | For Small Business | Compare Series

Campus LAN – Core and Distribution Switches
Scale network performance and reliability with industry- leading network services, integrated service
modules, and validated design guides.

Show Products ⊞

Campus LAN – Access Switches
Adapt your network to meet evolving business requirements and optimize new application
deployments with Cisco access switches.

Show Products ⊞

Campus LAN – Compact Switches
Securely and easily deploy services anywhere. These fanless, sleek, compact switches are ideal for
spaces with limited wiring and cabling infrastructure, such as kiosks, conference rooms, and call
centers.

Show Products ⊞

a. Click the heading **Campus LAN – Core and Distribution Switches**.

List a few models and some of features in the table below.

Model	Uplink Speed	Number of Ports/Speed	Other Features

b. Click the heading **Campus LAN – Access Switches**.

List a few models and some of features in the table below.

Model	Uplink Speed	Number of Ports/Speed	Other Features

c. Click the heading **Campus LAN – Compact Switches**.

List a few models and some of features in the table below.

Model	Uplink Speed	Number of Ports/Speed	Other Features

Part 2:   Select an Access Layer Switch

The main function of an access layer switch is to provide network access to end user devices. This switch connects to the core/distribution layer switches. Access switches are usually located in the intermediate distribution frame (IDF). An IDF is mainly used for managing and interconnecting the telecommunications cables between end user devices and a main distribution frame (MDF). There are typically multiple IDFs with uplinks to a single centralized MDF.

An access switch should have the following capabilities: low cost per switch port, high port density, scalable uplinks to higher layers, and user access functions and resiliency. In Part 2, you will select an access switch based on the requirements set by the company. You have reviewed and become familiar with Cisco switch product line.

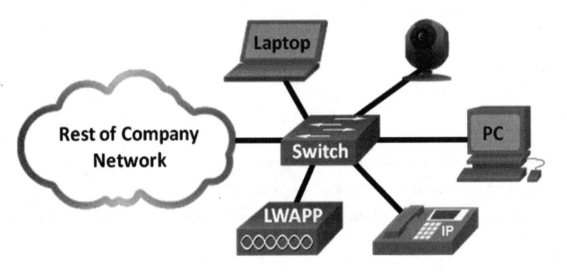

a. Company A requires a replacement access switch in the wiring closet. The company requires the switch to support VoIP and multicast, accommodate future growth of users and increased bandwidth usage. The switch must support a minimum of 35 current users and have a high-speed uplink. List a few of models that meet those requirements.

_____

_____

b.   Company B would like to extend services to a conference room on an as-needed basis. The switch will be placed on the conference room table, and switch security is a priority.

_____

_____

Part 3:   Select a Distribution/Core Layer Switch

The distribution/core switch is the backbone of the network for the company. A reliable network core is of paramount importance for the function of the company. A network backbone switch provides both adequate capacity for current and future traffic requirements and resilience in the event of failure. They also require high throughput, high availability, and advanced quality of service (QoS). These switches usually reside in the main wiring closet (MDF) along with high speed servers, routers, and the termination point of your ISP.

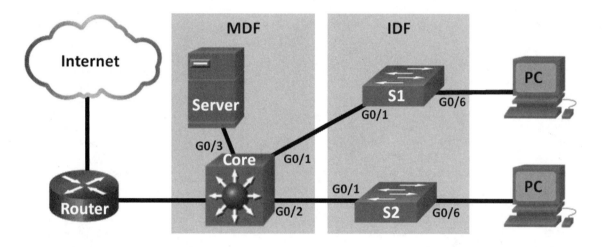

a.   Company C will replace a backbone switch in the next budget cycle. The switch must provide redundancy features to minimize possible downtime in the event that an internal component fails. What features can accommodate these requirements for the replacement switch?

_____

_____

b.   Which Cisco Catalyst switches would you recommend?

_____

c.   As Company C grows, high speed, such as 10 GB Ethernet, up to 8 uplink ports, and a modular configuration for the switch will become necessary. Which switch models would meet the requirement?

_____

Reflection

What other factors should be considered during the selection process aside from network requirements and costs?

_____

_____

1.3.1.1 Class Activity – It's Network Access Time

Objectives

Describe features available for switches to support requirements of a small- to medium-sized business network.

Scenario

Use Packet Tracer for this activity. Work with a classmate to create two network designs to accommodate the following scenarios:

Scenario 1 – Classroom Design (LAN)

- 15 student end devices represented by 1 or 2 PCs.

- 1 instructor end device; a server is preferred.

- Device capability to stream video presentations over LAN connection. Internet connectivity is not required in this design.

Scenario 2 – Administrative Design (WAN)

- All requirements as listed in Scenario 1.

- Add access to and from a remote administrative server for video presentations and pushed updates for network application software.

Both the LAN and WAN designs should fit on to one Packet Tracer file screen. All intermediary devices should be labeled with the switch model (or name) and the router model (or name).

Save your work and be ready to justify your device decisions and layout to your instructor and the class.

Reflection

1. What are some problems that may be encountered if you receive streaming video from your instructor's server through a low-end switch?

   _____

2. How would the traffic flow be determined: multicast or broadcast – in transmission?

   _____

3. What would influence your decision on the type of switch to use for voice, streaming video and regular data transmissions?

   _____

4. As you learned in the first course of the Academy, video and voice use a special TCP/IP model, transport layer protocol. What protocol is used in this layer and why is it important to voice and video streaming?

   _____

Chapter 2 — Basic Switching Concepts and Configuration

2.0.1.2 Class Activity – Stand By Me

Objective

Describe the role of unicast, broadcast, and multicast in a switched network.

Scenario

When you arrived to class today, you were given a number by your instructor to use for this introductory class activity.

Once class begins, your instructor will ask certain students with specific numbers to stand. Your job is to record the standing students' numbers for each scenario.

Scenario 1

Students with numbers **starting** with the number **5** should stand. Record the numbers of the standing students.

Scenario 2

Students with numbers **ending** in **B** should stand. Record the numbers of the standing students.

Scenario 3

The student with the number **505C** should stand. Record the number of the standing student.

At the end of this activity, divide into small groups and record answers to the Reflection questions on the PDF for this activity.

Reflection

1. Why do you think you were asked to record the students' numbers when and as requested?

_____

2. What is the significance of the number 5 in this activity? How many people were identified with this number?

_____

3. What is the significance of the letter B in this activity? How many people were identified with this number?

_____

4. Why did only one person stand for 505C?

_____

5. How do you think this activity represents data travelling on local area networks?

_____

Save your work and be prepared to share it with another student or the entire class.

2.1.1.6 Lab – Configuring Basic Switch Settings

Topology

Addressing Table

Device	Interface	IP Address	Subnet Mask	Default Gateway
S1	VLAN 99	192.168.1.2	255.255.255.0	192.168.1.1
PC-A	NIC	192.168.1.10	255.255.255.0	192.168.1.1

Objectives

Part 1: Cable the Network and Verify the Default Switch Configuration

Part 2: Configure Basic Network Device Settings

- Configure basic switch settings.
- Configure the PC IP address.

Part 3: Verify and Test Network Connectivity

- Display device configuration.
- Test end-to-end connectivity with ping.
- Test remote management capabilities with Telnet.
- Save the switch running configuration file.

Part 4: Manage the MAC Address Table

- Record the MAC address of the host.
- Determine the MAC addresses that the switch has learned.
- List the **show mac address-table** command options.
- Set up a static MAC address.

Background / Scenario

Cisco switches can be configured with a special IP address known as switch virtual interface (SVI). The SVI or management address can be used for remote access to the switch to display or configure settings. If the VLAN 1 SVI is assigned an IP address, by default, all ports in VLAN 1 have access to the SVI management IP address.

In this lab, you will build a simple topology using Ethernet LAN cabling and access a Cisco switch using the console and remote access methods. You will examine default switch configurations before configuring basic switch settings. These basic switch settings include device name, interface description, local passwords, message of the day (MOTD) banner, IP addressing, setting up a static MAC address, and demonstrating the use of a management IP address for remote switch management. The topology consists of one switch and one host using only Ethernet and console ports.

Note: The switch used is a Cisco Catalyst 2960 with Cisco IOS Release 15.0(2) (lanbasek9 image). Other switches and Cisco IOS versions can be used. Depending on the model and Cisco IOS version, the commands available and output produced might vary from what is shown in the labs.

Note: Make sure that the switch has been erased and has no startup configuration. Refer to Appendix A for the procedures to initialize and reload devices.

Required Resources

- 1 Switch (Cisco 2960 with Cisco IOS Release 15.0(2) lanbasek9 image or comparable)
- 1 PC (Windows 7, Vista, or XP with terminal emulation program, such as Tera Term, and Telnet capability)
- Console cable to configure the Cisco IOS device via the console port
- Ethernet cable as shown in the topology

Part 1:   Cable the Network and Verify the Default Switch Configuration

In Part 1, you will set up the network topology and verify default switch settings.

Step 1: Cable the network as shown in the topology.

a. Cable the console connection as shown in the topology. Do not connect the PC-A Ethernet cable at this time.

    Note: If you are using Netlab, you can shut down F0/6 on S1 which has the same effect as not connecting PC-A to S1.

b. Create a console connection to the switch from PC-A using Tera Term or other terminal emulation program.

    Why must you use a console connection to initially configure the switch? Why is it not possible to connect to the switch via Telnet or SSH?

    _____

Step 2:   Verify the default switch configuration.

In this step, you will examine the default switch settings, such as current switch configuration, IOS information, interface properties, VLAN information, and flash memory.

You can access all the switch IOS commands in privileged EXEC mode. Access to privileged EXEC mode should be restricted by password protection to prevent unauthorized use because it provides direct access to global configuration mode and commands used to configure operating parameters. You will set passwords later in this lab.

The privileged EXEC mode command set includes those commands contained in user EXEC mode, as well as the **configure** command through which access to the remaining command modes is gained. Use the **enable** command to enter privileged EXEC mode.

a. Assuming the switch had no configuration file stored in nonvolatile random-access memory (NVRAM), you will be at the user EXEC mode prompt on the switch with a prompt of Switch>. Use the **enable** command to enter privileged EXEC mode.

```
Switch> enable
Switch#
```

Notice that the prompt changed in the configuration to reflect privileged EXEC mode.

Verify a clean configuration file with the **show running-config** privileged EXEC mode command. If a configuration file was previously saved, it must be removed. Depending on switch model and IOS version, your configuration may look slightly different. However, there should be no configured passwords or IP address. If your switch does not have a default configuration, erase and reload the switch.

Note: Appendix A details the steps to initialize and reload the devices.

b.   Examine the current running configuration file.

```
Switch# show running-config
```

How many FastEthernet interfaces does a 2960 switch have? _____

How many Gigabit Ethernet interfaces does a 2960 switch have? _____

What is the range of values shown for the vty lines? _____

c.   Examine the startup configuration file in NVRAM.

```
Switch# show startup-config
startup-config is not present
```

Why does this message appear? _____

d.   Examine the characteristics of the SVI for VLAN 1.

```
Switch# show interface vlan1
```

Is there an IP address assigned to VLAN 1? _____

What is the MAC address of this SVI? Answers will vary. _____

Is this interface up?

_____

_____

e.   Examine the IP properties of the SVI VLAN 1.

```
Switch# show ip interface vlan1
```

What output do you see?

_____

_____

f.   Connect PC-A Ethernet cable to port 6 on the switch and examine the IP properties of the SVI VLAN 1. Allow time for the switch and PC to negotiate duplex and speed parameters.

Note: If you are using Netlab, enable interface F0/6 on S1.

```
Switch# show ip interface vlan1
```

What output do you see?

_____

_____

g. Examine the Cisco IOS version information of the switch.

    Switch# **show version**

    What is the Cisco IOS version that the switch is running? _____

    What is the system image filename? _____

    What is the base MAC address of this switch? Answers will vary. _____

h. Examine the default properties of the FastEthernet interface used by PC-A.

    Switch# **show interface f0/6**

    Is the interface up or down? _____

    What event would make an interface go up? _____

    What is the MAC address of the interface? _____

    What is the speed and duplex setting of the interface? _____

i. Examine the default VLAN settings of the switch.

    Switch# **show vlan**

    What is the default name of VLAN 1? _____

    Which ports are in this VLAN? _____

    Is VLAN 1 active? _____

    What type of VLAN is the default VLAN? _____

j. Examine flash memory.

    Issue one of the following commands to examine the contents of the flash directory.

    Switch# **show flash**

    Switch# **dir flash:**

    Files have a file extension, such as .bin, at the end of the filename. Directories do not have a file extension.

    What is the filename of the Cisco IOS image? _____

Part 2: Configure Basic Network Device Settings

In Part 2, you configure basic settings for the switch and PC.

Step 1: Configure basic switch settings including hostname, local passwords, MOTD banner, management address, and Telnet access.

In this step, you will configure the PC and basic switch settings, such as hostname and an IP address for the switch management SVI. Assigning an IP address on the switch is only the first step. As the network administrator, you must specify how the switch is managed. Telnet and SSH are the two most common management methods. However, Telnet is not a secure protocol. All information flowing between the two devices is sent in plain text. Passwords and other sensitive information can be easily looked at if captured by a packet sniffer.

a. Assuming the switch had no configuration file stored in NVRAM, verify you are at privileged EXEC mode. Enter **enable** if the prompt has changed back to Switch>.

```
Switch> enable
Switch#
```

b. Enter global configuration mode.

```
Switch# configure terminal
Enter configuration commands, one per line. End with CNTL/Z.
Switch(config)#
```

The prompt changed again to reflect global configuration mode.

c. Assign the switch hostname.

```
Switch(config)# hostname S1
S1(config)#
```

d. Configure password encryption.

```
S1(config)# service password-encryption
S1(config)#
```

e. Assign **class** as the secret password for privileged EXEC mode access.

```
S1(config)# enable secret class
S1(config)#
```

f. Prevent unwanted DNS lookups.

```
S1(config)# no ip domain-lookup
S1(config)#
```

g. Configure a MOTD banner.

```
S1(config)# banner motd #
Enter Text message.  End with the character '#'.
Unauthorized access is strictly prohibited. #
```

h. Verify your access settings by moving between modes.

```
S1(config)# exit
S1#
*Mar  1 00:19:19.490: %SYS-5-CONFIG_I: Configured from console by console
S1# exit

S1 con0 is now available


Press RETURN to get started.


Unauthorized access is strictly prohibited.
S1>
```

Which shortcut keys are used to go directly from global configuration mode to privileged EXEC mode?

_____

i. Go back to privileged EXEC mode from user EXEC mode. Enter **class** as the password when prompted.

```
S1> enable
Password:
S1#
```

Note: The password does not display when entering.

j. Enter global configuration mode to set the SVI IP address of the switch. This allows remote management of the switch.

Before you can manage S1 remotely from PC-A, you must assign the switch an IP address. The default configuration on the switch is to have the management of the switch controlled through VLAN 1. However, a best practice for basic switch configuration is to change the management VLAN to a VLAN other than VLAN 1.

For management purposes, use VLAN 99. The selection of VLAN 99 is arbitrary and in no way implies that you should always use VLAN 99.

First, create the new VLAN 99 on the switch. Then set the IP address of the switch to 192.168.1.2 with a subnet mask of 255.255.255.0 on the internal virtual interface VLAN 99.

```
S1# configure terminal
S1(config)# vlan 99
S1(config-vlan)# exit
S1(config)# interface vlan99
%LINEPROTO-5-UPDOWN: Line protocol on Interface Vlan99, changed state to down
S1(config-if)# ip address 192.168.1.2 255.255.255.0
S1(config-if)# no shutdown
S1(config-if)# exit
S1(config)#
```

Notice that the VLAN 99 interface is in the down state even though you entered the **no shutdown** command. The interface is currently down because no switch ports are assigned to VLAN 99.

k. Assign all user ports to VLAN 99.

```
S1(config)# interface range f0/1 - 24,g0/1 - 2
S1(config-if-range)# switchport access vlan 99
S1(config-if-range)# exit
S1(config)#
%LINEPROTO-5-UPDOWN: Line protocol on Interface Vlan1, changed state to down
%LINEPROTO-5-UPDOWN: Line protocol on Interface Vlan99, changed state to up
```

To establish connectivity between the host and the switch, the ports used by the host must be in the same VLAN as the switch. Notice in the above output that the VLAN 1 interface goes down because none of the ports are assigned to VLAN 1. After a few seconds, VLAN 99 comes up because at least one active port (F0/6 with PC-A attached) is now assigned to VLAN 99.

l. Issue **show vlan brief** command to verify that all the user ports are in VLAN 99.

```
S1# show vlan brief


VLAN Name                             Status    Ports
---- -------------------------------- --------- ------------------------------
1    default                          active
99   VLAN0099                         active    Fa0/1, Fa0/2, Fa0/3, Fa0/4
```

```
                                           Fa0/5, Fa0/6, Fa0/7, Fa0/8
                                           Fa0/9, Fa0/10, Fa0/11, Fa0/12
                                           Fa0/13, Fa0/14, Fa0/15, Fa0/16
                                           Fa0/17, Fa0/18, Fa0/19, Fa0/20
                                           Fa0/21, Fa0/22, Fa0/23, Fa0/24
                                           Gi0/1, Gi0/2
1002 fddi-default                  act/unsup
1003 token-ring-default            act/unsup
1004 fddinet-default               act/unsup
1005 trnet-default                 act/unsup
```

m. Configure the IP default gateway for S1. If no default gateway is set, the switch cannot be managed from a remote network that is more than one router away. It does respond to pings from a remote network. Although this activity does not include an external IP gateway, assume that you will eventually connect the LAN to a router for external access. Assuming that the LAN interface on the router is 192.168.1.1, set the default gateway for the switch.

```
S1(config)# ip default-gateway 192.168.1.1
S1(config)#
```

n. Console port access should also be restricted. The default configuration is to allow all console connections with no password needed. To prevent console messages from interrupting commands, use the **logging synchronous** option.

```
S1(config)# line con 0
S1(config-line)# password cisco
S1(config-line)# login
S1(config-line)# logging synchronous
S1(config-line)# exit
S1(config)#
```

o. Configure the virtual terminal (vty) lines for the switch to allow Telnet access. If you do not configure a vty password, you are unable to telnet to the switch.

```
S1(config)# line vty 0 15
S1(config-line)# password cisco
S1(config-line)# login
S1(config-line)# end
S1#
*Mar  1 00:06:11.590: %SYS-5-CONFIG_I: Configured from console by console
```

Why is the **login** command required? _____

Step 2:   Configure an IP address on PC-A.

Assign the IP address and subnet mask to the PC as shown in the Addressing Table. An abbreviated version of the procedure is described here. A default gateway is not required for this topology; however, you can enter **192.168.1.1** to simulate a router attached to S1.

1) Click the Windows **Start** icon > **Control Panel**.

2) Click **View By:** and choose **Small icons**.

3) Choose **Network and Sharing Center** > **Change adapter settings**.

4) Select **Local Area Network Connection,** right click and choose **Properties**.

5) Choose **Internet Protocol Version 4 (TCP/IPv4)** > **Properties**.

6) Click the **Use the following IP address** radio button and enter the IP address and subnet mask.

Part 3: Verify and Test Network Connectivity

In Part 3, you will verify and document the switch configuration, test end-to-end connectivity between PC-A and S1, and test the switch's remote management capability.

Step 1: Display the switch configuration.

From your console connection on PC-A, display and verify your switch configuration. The **show run** command displays the entire running configuration, one page at a time. Use the spacebar to advance paging.

a. A sample configuration displays here. The settings you configured are highlighted in yellow. The other configuration settings are IOS defaults.

```
S1# show run
Building configuration...

Current configuration : 2206 bytes
!
version 15.0
no service pad
service timestamps debug datetime msec
service timestamps log datetime msec
service password-encryption
!
hostname S1
!
boot-start-marker
boot-end-marker
!
enable secret 4 06YFDUHH61wAE/kLkDq9BGho1QM5EnRtoyr8cHAUg.2
!
no aaa new-model
system mtu routing 1500
!
!
no ip domain-lookup
!
<output omitted>
!
interface FastEthernet0/24
 switchport access vlan 99
!
interface GigabitEthernet0/1
!
interface GigabitEthernet0/2
!
interface Vlan1
 no ip address
 no ip route-cache
```

```
!
interface Vlan99
 ip address 192.168.1.2 255.255.255.0
 no ip route-cache
!
ip default-gateway 192.168.1.1
ip http server
ip http secure-server
!
banner motd ^C
Unauthorized access is strictly prohibited. ^C
!
line con 0
 password 7 104D000A0618
 logging synchronous
 login
line vty 0 4
 password 7 14141B180F0B
 login
line vty 5 15
 password 7 14141B180F0B
 login
!
end

S1#
```

b. Verify the management VLAN 99 settings.

```
S1# show interface vlan 99
Vlan99 is up, line protocol is up
  Hardware is EtherSVI, address is 0cd9.96e2.3d41 (bia 0cd9.96e2.3d41)
  Internet address is 192.168.1.2/24
  MTU 1500 bytes, BW 1000000 Kbit, DLY 10 usec,
     reliability 255/255, txload 1/255, rxload 1/255
  Encapsulation ARPA, loopback not set
  ARP type: ARPA, ARP Timeout 04:00:00
  Last input 00:00:06, output 00:08:45, output hang never
  Last clearing of "show interface" counters never
  Input queue: 0/75/0/0 (size/max/drops/flushes); Total output drops: 0
  Queueing strategy: fifo
  Output queue: 0/40 (size/max)
  5 minute input rate 0 bits/sec, 0 packets/sec
  5 minute output rate 0 bits/sec, 0 packets/sec
     175 packets input, 22989 bytes, 0 no buffer
     Received 0 broadcasts (0 IP multicast)
     0 runts, 0 giants, 0 throttles
     0 input errors, 0 CRC, 0 frame, 0 overrun, 0 ignored
     1 packets output, 64 bytes, 0 underruns
     0 output errors, 0 interface resets
     0 output buffer failures, 0 output buffers swapped out
```

What is the bandwidth on this interface? _____

What is the VLAN 99 state? _____

What is the line protocol state? _____

Step 2: Test end-to-end connectivity with ping.

a. From the command prompt on PC-A, ping your own PC-A address first.

    `C:\Users\User1>` **`ping 192.168.1.10`**

b. From the command prompt on PC-A, ping the SVI management address of S1.

    `C:\Users\User1>` **`ping 192.168.1.2`**

Because PC-A needs to resolve the MAC address of S1 through ARP, the first packet may time out. If ping results continue to be unsuccessful, troubleshoot the basic device configurations. You should check both the physical cabling and logical addressing if necessary.

Step 3: Test and verify remote management of S1.

You will now use Telnet to remotely access the switch. In this lab, PC-A and S1 reside side by side. In a production network, the switch could be in a wiring closet on the top floor while your management PC is located on the ground floor. In this step, you will use Telnet to remotely access switch S1 using its SVI management address. Telnet is not a secure protocol; however, you will use it to test remote access. With Telnet, all information, including passwords and commands, are sent across the session in plain text. In subsequent labs, you will use SSH to remotely access network devices.

Note: If you are using Windows 7, the administrator may need to enable the Telnet protocol. To install the Telnet client, open a cmd window and type **pkgmgr /iu:"TelnetClient"**. An example is shown below.

    `C:\Users\User1>` **`pkgmgr /iu:"TelnetClient"`**

a. With the cmd window still open on PC-A, issue a Telnet command to connect to S1 via the SVI management address. The password is **cisco**.

    `C:\Users\User1>` **`telnet 192.168.1.2`**

b. After entering the password **cisco**, you will be at the user EXEC mode prompt. Access privileged EXEC mode.

c. Type **exit** to end the Telnet session.

Step 4: Save the switch running configuration file.

Save the configuration.

    S1# **copy running-config startup-config**
    Destination filename [startup-config]? **[Enter]**
    Building configuration...
    [OK]
    S1#

Part 4: Manage the MAC Address Table

In Part 4, you will determine the MAC address that the switch has learned, set up a static MAC address on one interface of the switch, and then remove the static MAC address from that interface.

Step 1:   Record the MAC address of the host.

From a command prompt on PC-A, issue **ipconfig /all** command to determine and record the Layer 2 (physical) addresses of the PC NIC.

_____

Step 2:   Determine the MAC addresses that the switch has learned.

Display the MAC addresses using the **show mac address-table** command.

```
S1# show mac address-table
```

How many dynamic addresses are there? _____

How many MAC addresses are there in total? _____

Does the dynamic MAC address match the PC-A MAC address? _____

Step 3:   List the show mac address-table options.

a. Display the MAC address table options.
```
S1# show mac address-table ?
```

How many options are available for the **show mac address-table** command? _____

b. Issue the **show mac address-table dynamic** command to display only the MAC addresses that were learned dynamically.
```
S1# show mac address-table dynamic
```

How many dynamic addresses are there? _____

c. View the MAC address entry for PC-A. The MAC address formatting for the command is xxxx.xxxx.xxxx.
```
S1# show mac address-table address <PC-A MAC here>
```

Step 4:   Set up a static MAC address.

a. Clear the MAC address table.

To remove the existing MAC addresses, use the **clear mac address-table dynamic** command from privileged EXEC mode.
```
S1# clear mac address-table dynamic
```

b. Verify that the MAC address table was cleared.
```
S1# show mac address-table
```

How many static MAC addresses are there? _____

How many dynamic addresses are there? _____

c.   Examine the MAC table again.

More than likely, an application running on your PC has already sent a frame out the NIC to S1. Look at the MAC address table again in privileged EXEC mode to see if S1 has relearned the MAC address for PC-A.

S1# **show mac address-table**

How many dynamic addresses are there? _____

Why did this change from the last display? _____

If S1 has not yet relearned the MAC address for PC-A, ping the VLAN 99 IP address of the switch from PC-A, and then repeat the **show mac address-table** command.

d.   Set up a static MAC address.

To specify which ports a host can connect to, one option is to create a static mapping of the host MAC address to a port.

Set up a static MAC address on F0/6 using the address that was recorded for PC-A in Part 4, Step 1. The MAC address 0050.56BE.6C89 is used as an example only. You must use the MAC address of your PC-A, which is different than the one given here as an example.

S1(config)# **mac address-table static 0050.56BE.6C89 vlan 99 interface fastethernet 0/6**

e.   Verify the MAC address table entries.

S1# **show mac address-table**

How many total MAC addresses are there? _____

How many static addresses are there? _____

f.   Remove the static MAC entry. Enter global configuration mode and remove the command by putting a **no** in front of the command string.

Note: The MAC address 0050.56BE.6C89 is used in the example only. Use the MAC address for your PC-A.

S1(config)# **no mac address-table static 0050.56BE.6C89 vlan 99 interface fastethernet 0/6**

g.   Verify that the static MAC address has been cleared.

S1# **show mac address-table**

How many total static MAC addresses are there? _____

Reflection

1. Why should you configure the vty lines for the switch?

2. Why change the default VLAN 1 to a different VLAN number?

3. How can you prevent passwords from being sent in plain text?

4. Why configure a static MAC address on a port interface?

Appendix A: Initializing and Reloading a Router and Switch

Step 1:   Initialize and reload the router.

a. Console into the router and enable privileged EXEC mode.

```
Router> enable
Router#
```

a. Enter the **erase startup-config** command to remove the startup configuration from NVRAM.

```
Router# erase startup-config
Erasing the nvram filesystem will remove all configuration files! Continue? [confirm]
[OK]
Erase of nvram: complete
Router#
```

b. Issue the **reload** command to remove an old configuration from memory. When prompted to Proceed with reload?, press Enter. (Pressing any other key aborts the reload.)

```
Router# reload
Proceed with reload? [confirm]
*Nov 29 18:28:09.923: %SYS-5-RELOAD: Reload requested by console. Reload Reason:
Reload Command.
```

Note: You may receive a prompt asking to save the running configuration prior to reloading the router. Respond by typing **no** and press Enter.

```
System configuration has been modified. Save? [yes/no]: no
```

c. After the router reloads, you are prompted to enter the initial configuration dialog. Enter **no** and press Enter.

```
Would you like to enter the initial configuration dialog? [yes/no]: no
```

d. Another prompt asks to terminate autoinstall. Respond by typing **yes** press Enter.

```
Would you like to terminate autoinstall? [yes]: yes
```

Step 2: Initialize and reload the switch.

a. Console into the switch and enter privileged EXEC mode.

```
Switch> enable
Switch#
```

b. Use the **show flash** command to determine if any VLANs have been created on the switch.

```
Switch# show flash
Directory of flash:/

    2  -rwx        1919   Mar 1 1993 00:06:33 +00:00  private-config.text
    3  -rwx        1632   Mar 1 1993 00:06:33 +00:00  config.text
    4  -rwx       13336   Mar 1 1993 00:06:33 +00:00  multiple-fs
    5  -rwx    11607161   Mar 1 1993 02:37:06 +00:00  c2960-lanbasek9-mz.150-2.SE.bin
    6  -rwx         616   Mar 1 1993 00:07:13 +00:00  vlan.dat

32514048 bytes total (20886528 bytes free)
Switch#
```

c. If the **vlan.dat** file was found in flash, then delete this file.

```
Switch# delete vlan.dat
Delete filename [vlan.dat]?
```

d. You are prompted to verify the filename. If you have entered the name correctly, press Enter; otherwise, you can change the filename.

e. You are prompted to confirm to delete this file. Press Enter to confirm.

```
Delete flash:/vlan.dat? [confirm]
Switch#
```

f. Use the **erase startup-config** command to erase the startup configuration file from NVRAM. You are prompted to remove the configuration file. Press Enter to confirm.

```
Switch# erase startup-config
Erasing the nvram filesystem will remove all configuration files! Continue? [confirm]
[OK]
Erase of nvram: complete
Switch#
```

g. Reload the switch to remove any old configuration information from memory. You will then receive a prompt to confirm to reload the switch. Press Enter to proceed.

```
Switch# reload
Proceed with reload? [confirm]
```

Note: You may receive a prompt to save the running configuration prior to reloading the switch. Respond by typing **no** and press Enter.

```
System configuration has been modified. Save? [yes/no]: no
```

h. After the switch reloads, you should see a prompt to enter the initial configuration dialog. Respond by entering **no** at the prompt and press Enter.

```
Would you like to enter the initial configuration dialog? [yes/no]: no
Switch>
```

2.2.4.11 Lab – Configuring Switch Security Features

Topology

Addressing Table

Device	Interface	IP Address	Subnet Mask	Default Gateway
R1	G0/1	172.16.99.1	255.255.255.0	N/A
S1	VLAN 99	172.16.99.11	255.255.255.0	172.16.99.1
PC-A	NIC	172.16.99.3	255.255.255.0	172.16.99.1

Objectives

Part 1: Set Up the Topology and Initialize Devices

Part 2: Configure Basic Device Settings and Verify Connectivity

Part 3: Configure and Verify SSH Access on S1

- Configure SSH access.
- Modify SSH parameters.
- Verify the SSH configuration.

Part 4: Configure and Verify Security Features on S1

- Configure and verify general security features.
- Configure and verify port security.

Background / Scenario

It is quite common to lock down access and install good security features on PCs and servers. It is important that your network infrastructure devices, such as switches and routers, are also configured with security features.

In this lab, you will follow some best practices for configuring security features on LAN switches. You will only allow SSH and secure HTTPS sessions. You will also configure and verify port security to lock out any device with a MAC address not recognized by the switch.

Note: The router used with CCNA hands-on labs is a Cisco 1941 Integrated Services Router (ISR) with Cisco IOS Release 15.2(4)M3 (universalk9 image). The switch used is a Cisco Catalyst 2960 with Cisco IOS Release 15.0(2) (lanbasek9 image). Other routers, switches, and Cisco IOS versions can be used. Depending on the model and Cisco IOS version, the commands available and output produced might vary from what is shown in the labs. Refer to the Router Interface Summary Table at the end of this lab for the correct interface identifiers.

Note: Make sure that the router and switch have been erased and have no startup configurations. If you are unsure, contact your instructor or refer to the previous lab for the procedures to initialize and reload devices.

Required Resources

- 1 Router (Cisco 1941 with Cisco IOS Release 15.2(4)M3 universal image or comparable)
- 1 Switch (Cisco 2960 with Cisco IOS Release 15.0(2) lanbasek9 image or comparable)
- 1 PC (Windows 7, Vista, or XP with terminal emulation program, such as Tera Term)
- Console cables to configure the Cisco IOS devices via the console ports
- Ethernet cables as shown in the topology

Part 1:   Set Up the Topology and Initialize Devices

In Part 1, you will set up the network topology and clear any configurations if necessary.

Step 1:   Cable the network as shown in the topology.

Step 2:   Initialize and reload the router and switch.

If configuration files were previously saved on the router or switch, initialize and reload these devices back to their basic configurations.

Part 2:   Configure Basic Device Settings and Verify Connectivity

In Part 2, you configure basic settings on the router, switch, and PC. Refer to the Topology and Addressing Table at the beginning of this lab for device names and address information.

Step 1:   Configure an IP address on PC-A.

Step 2:   Configure basic settings on R1.

a. Configure the device name.

b. Disable DNS lookup.

c. Configure interface IP address as shown in the Addressing Table.

d. Assign **class** as the privileged EXEC mode password.

e. Assign **cisco** as the console and vty password and enable login.

f. Encrypt plain text passwords.

g. Save the running configuration to startup configuration.

Step 3:   Configure basic settings on S1.

A good security practice is to assign the management IP address of the switch to a VLAN other than VLAN 1 (or any other data VLAN with end users). In this step, you will create VLAN 99 on the switch and assign it an IP address.

a.   Configure the device name.

b.   Disable DNS lookup.

c.   Assign **class** as the privileged EXEC mode password.

d.   Assign **cisco** as the console and vty password and then enable login.

e.   Configure a default gateway for S1 using the IP address of R1.

f.   Encrypt plain text passwords.

g.   Save the running configuration to startup configuration.

h.   Create VLAN 99 on the switch and name it **Management**.

```
S1(config)# vlan 99
S1(config-vlan)# name Management
S1(config-vlan)# exit
S1(config)#
```

i.   Configure the VLAN 99 management interface IP address, as shown in the Addressing Table, and enable the interface.

```
S1(config)# interface vlan 99
S1(config-if)# ip address 172.16.99.11 255.255.255.0
S1(config-if)# no shutdown
S1(config-if)# end
S1#
```

j.   Issue the **show vlan** command on S1. What is the status of VLAN 99? _____

k.   Issue the **show ip interface brief** command on S1. What is the status and protocol for management interface VLAN 99?

_____

Why is the protocol down, even though you issued the **no shutdown** command for interface VLAN 99?

_____

l.   Assign ports F0/5 and F0/6 to VLAN 99 on the switch.

```
S1# config t
S1(config)# interface f0/5
S1(config-if)# switchport mode access
S1(config-if)# switchport access vlan 99
S1(config-if)# interface f0/6
S1(config-if)# switchport mode access
S1(config-if)# switchport access vlan 99
S1(config-if)# end
```

m.   Issue the **show ip interface brief** command on S1. What is the status and protocol showing for interface VLAN 99? _____

Note: There may be a delay while the port states converge.

Step 4:   Verify connectivity between devices.

a.   From PC-A, ping the default gateway address on R1. Were your pings successful? _____

b.   From PC-A, ping the management address of S1. Were your pings successful? _____

c.   From S1, ping the default gateway address on R1. Were your pings successful? _____

d.   From PC-A, open a web browser and go to http://172.16.99.11. If it prompts you for a username and password, leave the username blank and use **class** for the password. If it prompts for secured connection, answer **No**. Were you able to access the web interface on S1? _____

e.   Close the browser session on PC-A.

Note: The non-secure web interface (HTTP server) on a Cisco 2960 switch is enabled by default. A common security measure is to disable this service, as described in Part 4.

Part 3:   Configure and Verify SSH Access on S1

Step 1:   Configure SSH access on S1.

a.   Enable SSH on S1. From global configuration mode, create a domain name of **CCNA-Lab.com**.

```
S1(config)# ip domain-name CCNA-Lab.com
```

b.   Create a local user database entry for use when connecting to the switch via SSH. The user should have administrative level access.

   Note: The password used here is NOT a strong password. It is merely being used for lab purposes.

```
S1(config)# username admin privilege 15 secret sshadmin
```

c.   Configure the transport input for the vty lines to allow SSH connections only, and use the local database for authentication.

```
S1(config)# line vty 0 15
S1(config-line)# transport input ssh
S1(config-line)# login local
S1(config-line)# exit
```

d.   Generate an RSA crypto key using a modulus of 1024 bits.

```
S1(config)# crypto key generate rsa modulus 1024
The name for the keys will be: S1.CCNA-Lab.com

% The key modulus size is 1024 bits
% Generating 1024 bit RSA keys, keys will be non-exportable...
[OK] (elapsed time was 3 seconds)

S1(config)#
S1(config)# end
```

e.   Verify the SSH configuration and answer the questions below.

```
S1# show ip ssh
```

What version of SSH is the switch using? _____

How many authentication attempts does SSH allow? _____

What is the default timeout setting for SSH? _____

Step 2: Modify the SSH configuration on S1.

Modify the default SSH configuration.

```
S1# config t
S1(config)# ip ssh time-out 75
S1(config)# ip ssh authentication-retries 2
```

How many authentication attempts does SSH allow? _____

What is the timeout setting for SSH? _____

Step 3: Verify the SSH configuration on S1.

a. Using SSH client software on PC-A (such as Tera Term), open an SSH connection to S1. If you receive a message on your SSH client regarding the host key, accept it. Log in with **admin** for username and **cisco** for the password.

Was the connection successful? _____

What prompt was displayed on S1? Why?

_____

_____

_____

b. Type **exit** to end the SSH session on S1.

Part 4: Configure and Verify Security Features on S1

In Part 4, you will shut down unused ports, turn off certain services running on the switch, and configure port security based on MAC addresses. Switches can be subject to MAC address table overflow attacks, MAC spoofing attacks, and unauthorized connections to switch ports. You will configure port security to limit the number of MAC addresses that can be learned on a switch port and disable the port if that number is exceeded.

Step 1: Configure general security features on S1.

a. Configure a message of the day (MOTD) banner on S1 with an appropriate security warning message.

b. Issue a **show ip interface brief** command on S1. What physical ports are up?

_____

c. Shut down all unused physical ports on the switch. Use the **interface range** command.

```
S1(config)# interface range f0/1 - 4
S1(config-if-range)# shutdown
S1(config-if-range)# interface range f0/7 - 24
S1(config-if-range)# shutdown
S1(config-if-range)# interface range g0/1 - 2
S1(config-if-range)# shutdown
S1(config-if-range)# end
S1#
```

d. Issue the **show ip interface brief** command on S1. What is the status of ports F0/1 to F0/4?

_____

e. Issue the **show ip http server status** command.

What is the HTTP server status? _____

What server port is it using? _____

What is the HTTP secure server status? _____

What secure server port is it using? _____

f. HTTP sessions send everything in plain text. You will disable the HTTP service running on S1.

```
S1(config)# no ip http server
```

g. From PC-A, open a web browser session to http://172.16.99.11. What was your result?

_____

h. From PC-A, open a secure web browser session at https://172.16.99.11. Accept the certificate. Log in with no username and a password of **class**. What was your result?

_____

i. Close the web session on PC-A.

Step 2:   Configure and verify port security on S1.

a.   Record the R1 G0/1 MAC address. From the R1 CLI, use the **show interface g0/1** command and record the MAC address of the interface.

```
R1# show interface g0/1
GigabitEthernet0/1 is up, line protocol is up
  Hardware is CN Gigabit Ethernet, address is 30f7.0da3.1821 (bia
3047.0da3.1821)
```

What is the MAC address of the R1 G0/1 interface?

_____

b.   From the S1 CLI, issue a **show mac address-table** command from privileged EXEC mode. Find the dynamic entries for ports F0/5 and F0/6. Record them below.

F0/5 MAC address: _____

F0/6 MAC address: _____

c.   Configure basic port security.

Note: This procedure would normally be performed on all access ports on the switch. F0/5 is shown here as an example.

1) From the S1 CLI, enter interface configuration mode for the port that connects to R1.

```
S1(config)# interface f0/5
```

2) Shut down the port.

```
S1(config-if)# shutdown
```

3) Enable port security on F0/5.

```
S1(config-if)# switchport port-security
```

Note: Entering the **switchport port-security** command sets the maximum MAC addresses to 1 and the violation action to shutdown. The **switchport port-security maximum** and **switchport port-security violation** commands can be used to change the default behavior.

4) Configure a static entry for the MAC address of R1 G0/1 interface recorded in Step 2a.

```
S1(config-if)# switchport port-security mac-address xxxx.xxxx.xxxx
```

(xxxx.xxxx.xxxx is the actual MAC address of the router G0/1 interface)

Note: Optionally, you can use the `switchport port-security mac-address sticky` command to add all the secure MAC addresses that are dynamically learned on a port (up to the maximum set) to the switch running configuration.

5) Enable the switch port.

```
S1(config-if)# no shutdown
S1(config-if)# end
```

d.   Verify port security on S1 F0/5 by issuing a **show port-security interface** command.

```
S1# show port-security interface f0/5
Port Security              : Enabled
Port Status                : Secure-up
Violation Mode             : Shutdown
Aging Time                 : 0 mins
Aging Type                 : Absolute
SecureStatic Address Aging : Disabled
```

```
Maximum MAC Addresses        : 1
Total MAC Addresses          : 1
Configured MAC Addresses     : 1
Sticky MAC Addresses         : 0
Last Source Address:Vlan     : 0000.0000.0000:0
Security Violation Count     : 0
```

What is the port status of F0/5?

_____

e. From R1 command prompt, ping PC-A to verify connectivity.

```
R1# ping 172.16.99.3
```

f. You will now violate security by changing the MAC address on the router interface. Enter interface configuration mode for G0/1 and shut it down.

```
R1# config t
R1(config)# interface g0/1
R1(config-if)# shutdown
```

g. Configure a new MAC address for the interface, using **aaaa.bbbb.cccc** as the address.

```
R1(config-if)# mac-address aaaa.bbbb.cccc
```

h. If possible, have a console connection open on S1 at the same time that you do this step. You will see various messages displayed on the console connection to S1 indicating a security violation. Enable the G0/1 interface on R1.

```
R1(config-if)# no shutdown
```

i. From R1 privileged EXEC mode, ping PC-A. Was the ping successful? Why or why not?

_____

j. On the switch, verify port security with the following commands shown below.

```
S1# show port-security
Secure Port MaxSecureAddr CurrentAddr SecurityViolation Security Action
               (Count)       (Count)       (Count)
---------------------------------------------------------------------
     Fa0/5          1             1             1          Shutdown
---------------------------------------------------------------------
Total Addresses in System (excluding one mac per port)    :0
Max Addresses limit in System (excluding one mac per port) :8192


S1# show port-security interface f0/5
Port Security              : Enabled
Port Status                : Secure-shutdown
Violation Mode             : Shutdown
Aging Time                 : 0 mins
Aging Type                 : Absolute
SecureStatic Address Aging : Disabled
Maximum MAC Addresses      : 1
Total MAC Addresses        : 1
Configured MAC Addresses   : 1
Sticky MAC Addresses       : 0
Last Source Address:Vlan   : aaaa.bbbb.cccc:99
```

```
Security Violation Count   : 1
```

```
S1# show interface f0/5
FastEthernet0/5 is down, line protocol is down (err-disabled)
   Hardware is Fast Ethernet, address is 0cd9.96e2.3d05 (bia 0cd9.96e2.3d05)
   MTU 1500 bytes, BW 10000 Kbit/sec, DLY 1000 usec,
      reliability 255/255, txload 1/255, rxload 1/255
<output omitted>
```

```
S1# show port-security address
                 Secure Mac Address Table
--------------------------------------------------------------------

   Vlan    Mac Address        Type            Ports    Remaining Age
                                                       (mins)

   ----    ----------         ----            -----    -------------
    99     30f7.0da3.1821     SecureConfigured  Fa0/5    -
--------------------------------------------------------------------
Total Addresses in System (excluding one mac per port)    :0
Max Addresses limit in System (excluding one mac per port) :8192
```

k. On the router, shut down the G0/1 interface, remove the hard-coded MAC address from the router, and re-enable the G0/1 interface.

```
R1(config-if)# shutdown
R1(config-if)# no mac-address aaaa.bbbb.cccc
R1(config-if)# no shutdown
R1(config-if)# end
```

l. From R1, ping PC-A again at 172.16.99.3. Was the ping successful? _____

m. Issue the **show interface f0/5** command to determine the cause of ping failure. Record your findings.

_____

n. Clear the S1 F0/5 error disabled status.

```
S1# config t
S1(config)# interface f0/5
S1(config-if)# shutdown
S1(config-if)# no shutdown
```

Note: There may be a delay while the port states converge.

o. Issue the **show interface f0/5** command on S1 to verify F0/5 is no longer in error disabled mode.

```
S1# show interface f0/5
FastEthernet0/5 is up, line protocol is up (connected)
   Hardware is Fast Ethernet, address is 0023.5d59.9185 (bia 0023.5d59.9185)
   MTU 1500 bytes, BW 100000 Kbit/sec, DLY 100 usec,
      reliability 255/255, txload 1/255, rxload 1/255
```

p. From the R1 command prompt, ping PC-A again. You should be successful.

Reflection

1. Why would you enable port security on a switch?

2. Why should unused ports on a switch be disabled?

Router Interface Summary Table

Router Interface Summary				
Router Model	**Ethernet Interface #1**	**Ethernet Interface #2**	**Serial Interface #1**	**Serial Interface #2**
1800	Fast Ethernet 0/0 (F0/0)	Fast Ethernet 0/1 (F0/1)	Serial 0/0/0 (S0/0/0)	Serial 0/0/1 (S0/0/1)
1900	Gigabit Ethernet 0/0 (G0/0)	Gigabit Ethernet 0/1 (G0/1)	Serial 0/0/0 (S0/0/0)	Serial 0/0/1 (S0/0/1)
2801	Fast Ethernet 0/0 (F0/0)	Fast Ethernet 0/1 (F0/1)	Serial 0/1/0 (S0/1/0)	Serial 0/1/1 (S0/1/1)
2811	Fast Ethernet 0/0 (F0/0)	Fast Ethernet 0/1 (F0/1)	Serial 0/0/0 (S0/0/0)	Serial 0/0/1 (S0/0/1)
2900	Gigabit Ethernet 0/0 (G0/0)	Gigabit Ethernet 0/1 (G0/1)	Serial 0/0/0 (S0/0/0)	Serial 0/0/1 (S0/0/1)
Note: To find out how the router is configured, look at the interfaces to identify the type of router and how many interfaces the router has. There is no way to effectively list all the combinations of configurations for each router class. This table includes identifiers for the possible combinations of Ethernet and Serial interfaces in the device. The table does not include any other type of interface, even though a specific router may contain one. An example of this might be an ISDN BRI interface. The string in parenthesis is the legal abbreviation that can be used in Cisco IOS commands to represent the interface.				

2.3.1.1 Class Activity – Switch Trio

Objective

Verify the Layer 2 configuration of a switch port connected to an end station.

Scenario

You are the network administrator for a small- to medium-sized business. Corporate headquarters for your business has mandated that on all switches in all offices, security must be implemented. The memorandum delivered to you this morning states:

> *"By Monday, April 18, 20xx, the first three ports of all configurable switches located in all offices must be secured with MAC addresses — one address will be reserved for the printer, one address will be reserved for the laptop in the office, and one address will be reserved for the office server.*
>
> *If a port's security is breached, we ask you to shut it down until the reason for the breach can be certified.*
>
> *Please implement this policy no later than the date stated in this memorandum. For questions, call 1.800.555.1212. Thank you. The Network Management Team"*

Work with a partner in the class and create a Packet Tracer example to test this new security policy. Once you have created your file, test it with, at least, one device to ensure it is operational or validated.

Save your work and be prepared to share it with the entire class.

Reflection

1. Why would one port on a switch be secured on a switch using these scenario parameters (and not all the ports on the same switch)?

    _____

2. Why would a network administrator use a network simulator to create, configure, and validate a security plan, instead of using the small- to medium-sized business' actual, physical equipment?

    _____

Chapter 3 — VLANs

3.0.1.2 Class Activity – Vacation Station

Objective

Explain the purpose of VLANs in a switched network.

Scenario

You have purchased a three floor vacation home at the beach for rental purposes. The floor plan is identical on each floor. Each floor offers one digital television for renters to use.

According to the local Internet service provider, only three stations may be offered within a television package. It is your job to decide which television packages you offer your guests.

- Divide the class into groups of three students per group.
- Choose three different stations to make one subscription package for each floor of your rental home.
- Complete the PDF for this activity.

Share your completed group-reflection answers with the class.

Television Station Subscription Package – Floor 1		
Local News	**Sports**	**Weather**
☐	☐	☐
Home Improvement	**Movies**	**History**
☐	☐	☐
Television Station Subscription Package – Floor 2		
Local News	**Sports**	**Weather**
☐	☐	☐
Home Improvement	**Movies**	**History**
☐	☐	☐
Television Station Subscription Package – Floor 3		
Local News	**Sports**	**Weather**
☐	☐	☐
Home Improvement	**Movies**	**History**
☐	☐	☐

Reflection

1. What were some of the criteria you used to select the final three stations?

   _____

2. Why do you think this Internet service provider offers different television station options to subscribers? Why not offer all stations to all subscribers?

   _____

3. Compare this scenario to data communications and networks for small- to medium-sized businesses. Why would it be a good idea to divide your small- to medium-sized business networks into logical and physical groups?

   _____

3.2.2.5 Lab - Configuring VLANs and Trunking

Topology

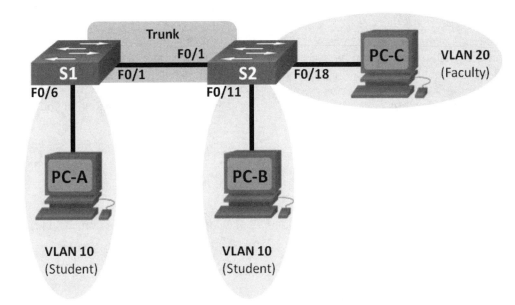

Addressing Table

Device	Interface	IP Address	Subnet Mask	Default Gateway
S1	VLAN 1	192.168.1.11	255.255.255.0	N/A
S2	VLAN 1	192.168.1.12	255.255.255.0	N/A
PC-A	NIC	192.168.10.3	255.255.255.0	192.168.10.1
PC-B	NIC	192.168.10.4	255.255.255.0	192.168.10.1
PC-C	NIC	192.168.20.3	255.255.255.0	192.168.20.1

Objectives

Part 1: Build the Network and Configure Basic Device Settings

Part 2: Create VLANs and Assign Switch Ports

Part 3: Maintain VLAN Port Assignments and the VLAN Database

Part 4: Configure an 802.1Q Trunk between the Switches

Part 5: Delete the VLAN Database

Background / Scenario

Modern switches use virtual local-area networks (VLANs) to improve network performance by separating large Layer 2 broadcast domains into smaller ones. VLANs can also be used as a security measure by controlling which hosts can communicate. In general, VLANs make it easier to design a network to support the goals of an organization.

VLAN trunks are used to span VLANs across multiple devices. Trunks allow the traffic from multiple VLANS to travel over a single link, while keeping the VLAN identification and segmentation intact.

In this lab, you will create VLANs on both switches in the topology, assign VLANs to switch access ports, verify that VLANs are working as expected, and then create a VLAN trunk between the two switches to allow hosts in the same VLAN to communicate through the trunk, regardless of which switch the host is actually attached to.

Note: The switches used are Cisco Catalyst 2960s with Cisco IOS Release 15.0(2) (lanbasek9 image). Other switches and Cisco IOS versions can be used. Depending on the model and Cisco IOS version, the commands available and output produced might vary from what is shown in the labs.

Note: Ensure that the switches have been erased and have no startup configurations. If you are unsure contact your instructor.

Required Resources

- 2 Switches (Cisco 2960 with Cisco IOS Release 15.0(2) lanbasek9 image or comparable)
- 3 PCs (Windows 7, Vista, or XP with terminal emulation program, such as Tera Term)
- Console cables to configure the Cisco IOS devices via the console ports
- Ethernet cables as shown in the topology

Part 1:   Build the Network and Configure Basic Device Settings

In Part 1, you will set up the network topology and configure basic settings on the PC hosts and switches.

Step 1:   Cable the network as shown in the topology.

Attach the devices as shown in the topology diagram, and cable as necessary.

Step 2:   Initialize and reload the switches as necessary.

Step 3:   Configure basic settings for each switch.

a.   Disable DNS lookup.

b.   Configure device name as shown in the topology.

c.   Assign **class** as the privileged EXEC password.

d.   Assign **cisco** as the console and vty passwords and enable login for console and vty lines.

e.   Configure **logging synchronous** for the console line.

f.   Configure a MOTD banner to warn users that unauthorized access is prohibited.

g.   Configure the IP address listed in the Addressing Table for VLAN 1 on both switches.

h.   Administratively deactivate all unused ports on the switch.

i.   Copy the running configuration to the startup configuration.

Step 4:   Configure PC hosts.

Refer to the Addressing Table for PC host address information.

Step 5:   Test connectivity.

Verify that the PC hosts can ping one another.

Note: It may be necessary to disable the PCs firewall to ping between PCs.

Can PC-A ping PC-B? _____

Can PC-A ping PC-C? _____

Can PC-A ping S1?   _____

Can PC-B ping PC-C? _____

Can PC-B ping S2?   _____

Can PC-C ping S2?   _____

Can S1 ping S2?   _____

If you answered no to any of the above questions, why were the pings unsuccessful?

_____

_____

Part 2:   Create VLANs and Assign Switch Ports

In Part 2, you will create student, faculty, and management VLANs on both switches. You will then assign the VLANs to the appropriate interface. The **show vlan** command is used to verify your configuration settings.

Step 1:   Create VLANs on the switches.

a.   Create the VLANs on S1.

```
S1(config)# vlan 10
S1(config-vlan)# name Student
S1(config-vlan)# vlan 20
S1(config-vlan)# name Faculty
S1(config-vlan)# vlan 99
S1(config-vlan)# name Management
S1(config-vlan)# end
```

b.   Create the same VLANs on S2.

c.   Issue the **show vlan** command to view the list of VLANs on S1.

```
S1# show vlan
```

```
VLAN Name                             Status    Ports
---- -------------------------------- --------- -------------------------------
1    default                          active    Fa0/1, Fa0/2, Fa0/3, Fa0/4
                                                Fa0/5, Fa0/6, Fa0/7, Fa0/8
                                                Fa0/9, Fa0/10, Fa0/11, Fa0/12
```

```
                                        Fa0/13, Fa0/14, Fa0/15, Fa0/16
                                        Fa0/17, Fa0/18, Fa0/19, Fa0/20
                                        Fa0/21, Fa0/22, Fa0/23, Fa0/24
                                        Gi0/1, Gi0/2

10    Student                           active
20    Faculty                           active
99    Management                        active
1002  fddi-default                      act/unsup
1003  token-ring-default                act/unsup
1004  fddinet-default                   act/unsup
1005  trnet-default                     act/unsup


VLAN Type  SAID       MTU   Parent RingNo BridgeNo Stp  BrdgMode Trans1 Trans2
---- ----- ---------- ----- ------ ------ -------- ---- -------- ------ ------
1    enet  100001     1500  -      -      -        -    -        0      0
10   enet  100010     1500  -      -      -        -    -        0      0
20   enet  100020     1500  -      -      -        -    -        0      0
99   enet  100099     1500  -      -      -        -    -        0      0


VLAN Type  SAID       MTU   Parent RingNo BridgeNo Stp  BrdgMode Trans1 Trans2
---- ----- ---------- ----- ------ ------ -------- ---- -------- ------ ------
1002 fddi  101002     1500  -      -      -        -    -        0      0
1003 tr    101003     1500  -      -      -        -    -        0      0
1004 fdnet 101004     1500  -      -      -        ieee -        0      0
1005 trnet 101005     1500  -      -      -        ibm  -        0      0


Remote SPAN VLANs
-------------------------------------------------------------------------------



Primary Secondary Type              Ports
------- --------- ----------------- ---------------------------------------
```

What is the default VLAN? _____

What ports are assigned to the default VLAN?

_____

Step 2: Assign VLANs to the correct switch interfaces.

a. Assign VLANs to the interfaces on S1.

1) Assign PC-A to the Student VLAN.

```
S1(config)# interface f0/6
S1(config-if)# switchport mode access
S1(config-if)# switchport access vlan 10
```

2) Move the switch IP address VLAN 99.

```
S1(config)# interface vlan 1
S1(config-if)# no ip address
S1(config-if)# interface vlan 99
```

```
S1(config-if)# ip address 192.168.1.11 255.255.255.0
S1(config-if)# end
```

b. Issue the **show vlan brief** command and verify that the VLANs are assigned to the correct interfaces.

```
S1# show vlan brief

VLAN Name                             Status    Ports
---- -------------------------------- --------- -------------------------------
1    default                          active    Fa0/1, Fa0/2, Fa0/3, Fa0/4
                                                Fa0/5, Fa0/7, Fa0/8, Fa0/9
                                                Fa0/10, Fa0/11, Fa0/12, Fa0/13
                                                Fa0/14, Fa0/15, Fa0/16, Fa0/17
                                                Fa0/18, Fa0/19, Fa0/20, Fa0/21
                                                Fa0/22, Fa0/23, Fa0/24, Gi0/1
                                                Gi0/2
10   Student                          active    Fa0/6
20   Faculty                          active
99   Management                       active
1002 fddi-default                     act/unsup
1003 token-ring-default               act/unsup
1004 fddinet-default                  act/unsup
1005 trnet-default                    act/unsup
```

c. Issue the **show ip interface brief** command.

What is the status of VLAN 99? Why?

_____

d. Use the Topology to assign VLANs to the appropriate ports on S2.

e. Remove the IP address for VLAN 1 on S2.

f. Configure an IP address for VLAN 99 on S2 according to the Addressing Table.

g. Use the **show vlan brief** command to verify that the VLANs are assigned to the correct interfaces.

```
S2# show vlan brief

VLAN Name                             Status    Ports
---- -------------------------------- --------- -------------------------------
1    default                          active    Fa0/1, Fa0/2, Fa0/3, Fa0/4
                                                Fa0/5, Fa0/6, Fa0/7, Fa0/8
                                                Fa0/9, Fa0/10, Fa0/12, Fa0/13
                                                Fa0/14, Fa0/15, Fa0/16, Fa0/17
                                                Fa0/19, Fa0/20, Fa0/21, Fa0/22
                                                Fa0/23, Fa0/24, Gi0/1, Gi0/2
10   Student                          active    Fa0/11
20   Faculty                          active    Fa0/18
99   Management                       active
1002 fddi-default                     act/unsup
1003 token-ring-default               act/unsup
1004 fddinet-default                  act/unsup
1005 trnet-default                    act/unsup
```

Is PC-A able to ping PC-B? Why?

_____

Is S1 able to ping S2? Why?

_____

Part 3:   Maintain VLAN Port Assignments and the VLAN Database

In Part 3, you will change VLAN assignments to ports and remove VLANs from the VLAN database.

Step 1:   Assign a VLAN to multiple interfaces.

a.   On S1, assign interfaces F0/11 – 24 to VLAN 10.
```
S1(config)# interface range f0/11-24
S1(config-if-range)# switchport mode access
S1(config-if-range)# switchport access vlan 10
S1(config-if-range)# end
```
b.   Issue the **show vlan brief** command to verify VLAN assignments.

c.   Reassign F0/11 and F0/21 to VLAN 20.

d.   Verify that VLAN assignments are correct.

Step 2:   Remove a VLAN assignment from an interface.

a.   Use the **no switchport access vlan** command to remove the VLAN 10 assignment to F0/24.
```
S1(config)# interface f0/24
S1(config-if)# no switchport access vlan
S1(config-if)# end
```
b.   Verify that the VLAN change was made.

Which VLAN is F0/24 now associated with?

_____

Step 3:   Remove a VLAN ID from the VLAN database.

a.   Add VLAN 30 to interface F0/24 without issuing the VLAN command.
```
S1(config)# interface f0/24
S1(config-if)# switchport access vlan 30
% Access VLAN does not exist. Creating vlan 30
```

Note: Current switch technology no longer requires that the **vlan** command be issued to add a VLAN to the database. By assigning an unknown VLAN to a port, the VLAN adds to the VLAN database.

b.   Verify that the new VLAN is displayed in the VLAN table.
```
S1# show vlan brief
```

```
VLAN Name                             Status    Ports
---- -------------------------------- --------- -------------------------------
1    default                          active    Fa0/1, Fa0/2, Fa0/3, Fa0/4
                                                Fa0/5, Fa0/6, Fa0/7, Fa0/8
                                                Fa0/9, Fa0/10, Gi0/1, Gi0/2
10   Student                          active    Fa0/12, Fa0/13, Fa0/14, Fa0/15
                                                Fa0/16, Fa0/17, Fa0/18, Fa0/19
                                                Fa0/20, Fa0/22, Fa0/23
20   Faculty                          active    Fa0/11, Fa0/21
30   VLAN0030                         active    Fa0/24
99   Management                       active
1002 fddi-default                     act/unsup
1003 token-ring-default               act/unsup
1004 fddinet-default                  act/unsup
1005 trnet-default                    act/unsup
```

What is the default name of VLAN 30?

_____

c. Use the **no vlan 30** command to remove VLAN 30 from the VLAN database.

    S1(config)# **no vlan 30**

    S1(config)# **end**

d. Issue the **show vlan brief** command. F0/24 was assigned to VLAN 30.

    After deleting VLAN 30, what VLAN is port F0/24 assigned to? What happens to the traffic destined to the host attached to F0/24?

_____

S1# **show vlan brief**

```
VLAN Name                             Status    Ports
---- -------------------------------- --------- -------------------------------
1    default                          active    Fa0/1, Fa0/2, Fa0/3, Fa0/4
                                                Fa0/5, Fa0/6, Fa0/7, Fa0/8
                                                Fa0/9, Fa0/10, Gi0/1, Gi0/2
10   Student                          active    Fa0/12, Fa0/13, Fa0/14, Fa0/15
                                                Fa0/16, Fa0/17, Fa0/18, Fa0/19
                                                Fa0/20, Fa0/22, Fa0/23
20   Faculty                          active    Fa0/11, Fa0/21
99   Management                       active
1002 fddi-default                     act/unsup
1003 token-ring-default               act/unsup
1004 fddinet-default                  act/unsup
1005 trnet-default                    act/unsup
```

e.   Issue the **no switchport access vlan** command on interface F0/24.

f.   Issue the **show vlan brief** command to determine the VLAN assignment for F0/24. To which VLAN is F0/24 assigned?

_____

Note: Before removing a VLAN from the database, it is recommended that you reassign all the ports assigned to that VLAN.

Why should you reassign a port to another VLAN before removing the VLAN from the VLAN database?

_____

_____

_____

Part 4:   Configure an 802.1Q Trunk Between the Switches

In Part 4, you will configure interface F0/1 to use the Dynamic Trunking Protocol (DTP) to allow it to negotiate the trunk mode. After this has been accomplished and verified, you will disable DTP on interface F0/1 and manually configure it as a trunk.

Step 1:   Use DTP to initiate trunking on F0/1.

The default DTP mode of a 2960 switch port is dynamic auto. This allows the interface to convert the link to a trunk if the neighboring interface is set to trunk or dynamic desirable mode.

a.   Set F0/1 on S1 to negotiate trunk mode.

```
S1(config)# interface f0/1

S1(config-if)# switchport mode dynamic desirable

*Mar  1 05:07:28.746: %LINEPROTO-5-UPDOWN: Line protocol on Interface Vlan1, changed
state to down

*Mar  1 05:07:29.744: %LINEPROTO-5-UPDOWN: Line protocol on Interface FastEthernet0/1,
changed state to down

S1(config-if)#

*Mar  1 05:07:32.772: %LINEPROTO-5-UPDOWN: Line protocol on Interface FastEthernet0/1,
changed state to up

S1(config-if)#

*Mar  1 05:08:01.789: %LINEPROTO-5-UPDOWN: Line protocol on Interface Vlan99, changed
state to up

*Mar  1 05:08:01.797: %LINEPROTO-5-UPDOWN: Line protocol on Interface Vlan1, changed
state to up
```

You should also receive link status messages on S2.

```
S2#

*Mar  1 05:07:29.794: %LINEPROTO-5-UPDOWN: Line protocol on Interface FastEthernet0/1,
changed state to down

S2#

*Mar  1 05:07:32.823: %LINEPROTO-5-UPDOWN: Line protocol on Interface FastEthernet0/1,
changed state to up

S2#

*Mar  1 05:08:01.839: %LINEPROTO-5-UPDOWN: Line protocol on Interface Vlan99, changed
state to up

*Mar  1 05:08:01.850: %LINEPROTO-5-UPDOWN: Line protocol on Interface Vlan1, changed
state to up
```

b.   Issue the **show vlan brief** command on S1 and S2. Interface F0/1 is no longer assigned to VLAN 1. Trunked interfaces are not listed in the VLAN table.

```
S1# show vlan brief

VLAN Name                             Status    Ports
---- -------------------------------- --------- -------------------------------
1    default                          active    Fa0/2, Fa0/3, Fa0/4, Fa0/5
                                                Fa0/7, Fa0/8, Fa0/9, Fa0/10
                                                Fa0/24, Gi0/1, Gi0/2
10   Student                          active    Fa0/6, Fa0/12, Fa0/13, Fa0/14
                                                Fa0/15, Fa0/16, Fa0/17, Fa0/18
                                                Fa0/19, Fa0/20, Fa0/22, Fa0/23
20   Faculty                          active    Fa0/11, Fa0/21
99   Management                       active
1002 fddi-default                     act/unsup
1003 token-ring-default               act/unsup
1004 fddinet-default                  act/unsup
1005 trnet-default                    act/unsup
```

c. Issue the **show interfaces trunk** command to view trunked interfaces. Notice that the mode on S1 is set to desirable, and the mode on S2 is set to auto.

```
S1# show interfaces trunk

Port      Mode           Encapsulation  Status        Native vlan
Fa0/1     desirable      802.1q         trunking      1

Port      Vlans allowed on trunk
Fa0/1     1-4094

Port      Vlans allowed and active in management domain
Fa0/1     1,10,20,99

Port      Vlans in spanning tree forwarding state and not pruned
Fa0/1     1,10,20,99


S2# show interfaces trunk

Port      Mode           Encapsulation  Status        Native vlan
Fa0/1     auto           802.1q         trunking      1

Port      Vlans allowed on trunk
Fa0/1     1-4094

Port      Vlans allowed and active in management domain
Fa0/1     1,10,20,99

Port      Vlans in spanning tree forwarding state and not pruned
Fa0/1     1,10,20,99
```

Note: By default, all VLANs are allowed on a trunk. The **switchport trunk** command allows you to control what VLANs have access to the trunk. For this lab, keep the default settings which allows all VLANs to traverse F0/1.

d. Verify that VLAN traffic is traveling over trunk interface F0/1.

Can S1 ping S2? _____

Can PC-A ping PC-B? _____

Can PC-A ping PC-C? _____

Can PC-B ping PC-C? _____

Can PC-A ping S1? _____

Can PC-B ping S2? _____

Can PC-C ping S2? _____

If you answered no to any of the above questions, explain below.

_____

_____

Step 2: Manually configure trunk interface F0/1.

The **switchport mode trunk** command is used to manually configure a port as a trunk. This command should be issued on both ends of the link.

a. Change the switchport mode on interface F0/1 to force trunking. Make sure to do this on both switches.

```
S1(config)# interface f0/1
S1(config-if)# switchport mode trunk
```

b. Issue the **show interfaces trunk** command to view the trunk mode. Notice that the mode changed from **desirable** to **on**.

```
S2# show interfaces trunk
```

```
Port          Mode                Encapsulation  Status       Native vlan
Fa0/1         on                  802.1q         trunking     99


Port          Vlans allowed on trunk
Fa0/1         1-4094


Port          Vlans allowed and active in management domain
Fa0/1         1,10,20,99


Port          Vlans in spanning tree forwarding state and not pruned
Fa0/1         1,10,20,99
```

Why might you want to manually configure an interface to trunk mode instead of using DTP?

_____

_____

Part 5: Delete the VLAN Database

In Part 5, you will delete the VLAN Database from the switch. It is necessary to do this when initializing a switch back to its default settings.

Step 1: Determine if the VLAN database exists.

Issue the **show flash** command to determine if a **vlan.dat** file exists in flash.

```
S1# show flash

Directory of flash:/

    2   -rwx        1285    Mar 1 1993 00:01:24 +00:00  config.text
    3   -rwx       43032    Mar 1 1993 00:01:24 +00:00  multiple-fs
    4   -rwx           5    Mar 1 1993 00:01:24 +00:00  private-config.text
    5   -rwx    11607161    Mar 1 1993 02:37:06 +00:00  c2960-lanbasek9-mz.150-2.SE.bin
    6   -rwx         736    Mar 1 1993 00:19:41 +00:00  vlan.dat

32514048 bytes total (20858880 bytes free)
```

Note: If there is a **vlan.dat** file located in flash, then the VLAN database does not contain its default settings.

Step 2: Delete the VLAN database.

a. Issue the **delete vlan.dat** command to delete the vlan.dat file from flash and reset the VLAN database back to its default settings. You will be prompted twice to confirm that you want to delete the vlan.dat file. Press Enter both times.

```
S1# delete vlan.dat
Delete filename [vlan.dat]?
Delete flash:/vlan.dat? [confirm]
S1#
```

b. Issue the **show flash** command to verify that the vlan.dat file has been deleted.

```
S1# show flash

Directory of flash:/

    2   -rwx        1285    Mar 1 1993 00:01:24 +00:00  config.text
    3   -rwx       43032    Mar 1 1993 00:01:24 +00:00  multiple-fs
    4   -rwx           5    Mar 1 1993 00:01:24 +00:00  private-config.text
    5   -rwx    11607161    Mar 1 1993 02:37:06 +00:00  c2960-lanbasek9-mz.150-2.SE.bin

32514048 bytes total (20859904 bytes free)
```

To initialize a switch back to its default settings, what other commands are needed?

_____

_____

Reflection

1. What is needed to allow hosts on VLAN 10 to communicate to hosts on VLAN 20?

    _____

    _____

2. What are some primary benefits that an organization can receive through effective use of VLANs?

    _____

    _____

    _____

    _____

3.2.4.9 Lab - Troubleshooting VLAN Configurations

Topology

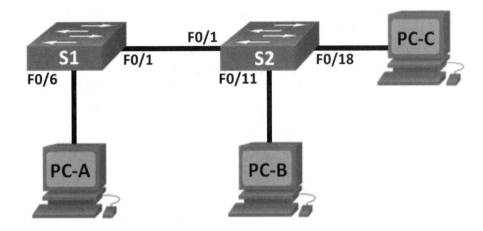

Addressing Table

Device	Interface	IP Address	Subnet Mask	Default Gateway
S1	VLAN 1	192.168.1.2	255.255.255.0	N/A
S2	VLAN 1	192.168.1.3	255.255.255.0	N/A
PC-A	NIC	192.168.10.2	255.255.255.0	192.168.10.1
PC-B	NIC	192.168.10.3	255.255.255.0	192.168.10.1
PC-C	NIC	192.168.20.3	255.255.255.0	192.168.20.1

Switch Port Assignment Specifications

Ports	Assignment	Network
F0/1	802.1Q Trunk	N/A
F0/6-12	VLAN 10 – Students	192.168.10.0/24
F0/13-18	VLAN 20 – Faculty	192.168.20.0/24
F0/19-24	VLAN 30 – Guest	192.168.30.0/24

Objectives

Part 1: Build the Network and Configure Basic Device Settings

Part 2: Troubleshoot VLAN 10

Part 3: Troubleshoot VLAN 20

Background / Scenario

VLANs provide logical segmentation within an internetwork and improve network performance by separating large broadcast domains into smaller ones. By separating hosts into different networks, VLANs can be used to control which hosts can communicate. In this lab, a school has decided to implement VLANs in order to separate traffic from different end users. The school is using 802.1Q trunking to facilitate VLAN communication between switches.

The S1 and S2 switches have been configured with VLAN and trunking information. Several errors in the configuration have resulted in connectivity issues. You have been asked to troubleshoot and correct the configuration errors and document your work.

Note: The switches used with this lab are Cisco Catalyst 2960s with Cisco IOS Release 15.0(2) (lanbasek9 image). Other switches and Cisco IOS versions can be used. Depending on the model and Cisco IOS version, the commands available and output produced might vary from what is shown in the labs.

Note: Make sure that the switches have been erased and have no startup configurations. If you are unsure, contact your instructor.

Required Resources

- 2 Switches (Cisco 2960 with Cisco IOS Release 15.0(2) lanbasek9 image or comparable)
- 3 PCs (Windows 7, Vista, or XP with terminal emulation program, such as Tera Term)
- Console cables to configure the Cisco IOS devices via the console ports
- Ethernet cables as shown in the topology

Part 1: Build the Network and Configure Basic Device Settings

In Part 1, you will set up the network topology and configure the switches with some basic settings, such as passwords and IP addresses. Preset VLAN-related configurations, which contain errors, are provided for you for the initial switch configurations. You will also configure the IP settings for the PCs in the topology.

Step 1:   Cable the network as shown in the topology.

Step 2:   Configure PC hosts.

Step 3:   Initialize and reload the switches as necessary.

Step 4:   Configure basic settings for each switch.

a. Disable DNS lookup.

b. Configure the IP address according to the Addressing Table.

c. Assign **cisco** as the console and vty passwords and enable login for console and vty lines.

d. Assign **class** as the privileged EXEC password.

e. Configure **logging synchronous** to prevent console messages from interrupting command entry.

Step 5:   Load switch configurations.

The configurations for the switches S1 and S2 are provided for you. There are errors within these configurations, and it is your job to determine the incorrect configurations and correct them.

Switch S1 Configuration:

```
hostname S1
vlan 10
 name Students
```

```
vlan 2

name Faculty
vlan 30
 name Guest
interface range f0/1-24
 switchport mode access
 shutdown




interface range f0/7-12

 switchport access vlan 10
interface range f0/13-18
 switchport access vlan 2

interface range f0/19-24
 switchport access vlan 30
end
```

Switch S2 Configuration:

```
hostname S2
vlan 10
 name Students
vlan 20
 name Faculty
vlan 30
 name Guest
interface f0/1
 switchport mode trunk
 switchport trunk allowed vlan 1,10,2,30

interface range f0/2-24
 switchport mode access
 shutdown



interface range f0/13-18
 switchport access vlan 20
interface range f0/19-24
 switchport access vlan 30
 shutdown
end
```

Step 6:   Copy the running configuration to the startup configuration.

Part 2:   Troubleshoot VLAN 10

In Part 2, you must examine VLAN 10 on S1 and S2 to determine if it is configured correctly. You will trouble-shoot the scenario until connectivity is established.

Step 1:   Troubleshoot VLAN 10 on S1.

a.   Can PC-A ping PC-B? _____

b.   After verifying that PC-A was configured correctly, examine the S1 switch to find possible configuration errors by viewing a summary of the VLAN information. Enter the **show vlan brief** command.

c.   Are there any problems with the VLAN configuration?

_____

d.   Examine the switch for trunk configurations using the **show interfaces trunk** and the **show interfaces f0/1 switchport** commands.

e.   Are there any problems with the trunking configuration?

_____

f.   Examine the running configuration of the switch to find possible configuration errors.

Are there any problems with the current configuration?

_____

g.   Correct the errors found regarding F0/1 and VLAN 10 on S1. Record the commands used in the space below.

_____

_____

_____

_____

h.   Verify the commands had the desired effects by issuing the appropriate **show** commands.

i.   Can PC-A ping PC-B? _____

Step 2:   Troubleshoot VLAN 10 on S2.

a.   Using the previous commands, examine the S2 switch to find possible configuration errors.

Are there any problems with the current configuration?

_____

b.   Correct the errors found regarding interfaces and VLAN 10 on S2. Record the commands below.

_____

_____

_____

_____

_____

c.   Can PC-A ping PC-B? _____

Part 3: Troubleshoot VLAN 20

In Part 3, you must examine VLAN 20 on S1 and S2 to determine if it is configured correctly. To verify functionality, you will reassign PC-A into VLAN 20, and then troubleshoot the scenario until connectivity is established.

Step 1: Assign PC-A to VLAN 20.

a. On PC-A, change the IP address to 192.168.20.2/24 with a default gateway of 192.168.20.1.

b. On S1, assign the port for PC-A to VLAN 20. Write the commands needed to complete the configuration.

_____

_____

c. Verify that the port for PC-A has been assigned to VLAN 20.

d. Can PC-A ping PC-C? _____

Step 2: Troubleshoot VLAN 20 on S1.

a. Using the previous commands, examine the S1 switch to find possible configuration errors.

Are there any problems with the current configuration?

_____

_____

a. Correct the errors found regarding VLAN 20.

b. Can PC-A ping PC-C? _____

Step 3: Troubleshoot VLAN 20 on S2.

a. Using the previous commands, examine the S2 switch to find possible configuration errors.

Are there any problems with the current configuration?

_____

b. Correct the errors found regarding VLAN 20. Record the commands used below.

_____

_____

_____

_____

_____

c. Can PC-A ping PC-C? _____

Note: It may be necessary to disable the PC firewall to ping between PCs.

Reflection

1. Why is a correctly configured trunk port critical in a multi-VLAN environment?

   _____

   _____

2. Why would a network administrator limit traffic for specific VLANs on a trunk port?

   _____

   _____

3.3.2.2 Lab – Implementing VLAN Security

Topology

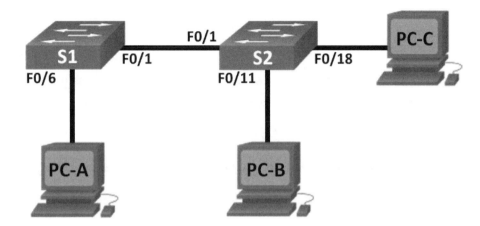

Addressing Table

Device	Interface	IP Address	Subnet Mask	Default Gateway
S1	VLAN 99	172.17.99.11	255.255.255.0	172.17.99.1
S2	VLAN 99	172.17.99.12	255.255.255.0	172.17.99.1
PC-A	NIC	172.17.99.3	255.255.255.0	172.17.99.1
PC-B	NIC	172.17.10.3	255.255.255.0	172.17.10.1
PC-C	NIC	172.17.99.4	255.255.255.0	172.17.99.1

VLAN Assignments

VLAN	Name
10	Data
99	Management&Native
999	BlackHole

Objectives

Part 1: Build the Network and Configure Basic Device Settings

Part 2: Implement VLAN Security on the Switches

Background / Scenario

Best practice dictates configuring some basic security settings for both access and trunk ports on switches. This will help guard against VLAN attacks and possible sniffing of network traffic within the network.

In this lab, you will configure the network devices in the topology with some basic settings, verify connectivity and then apply more stringent security measures on the switches. You will examine how Cisco switches behave by using various **show** commands. You will then apply security measures.

Note: The switches used with this lab are Cisco Catalyst 2960s with Cisco IOS Release 15.0(2) (lanbasek9 image). Other switches and Cisco IOS versions can be used. Depending on the model and Cisco IOS version, the commands available and output produced might vary from what is shown in the labs.

Note: Make sure that the switches have been erased and have no startup configurations. If you are unsure, contact your instructor.

Required Resources

- 2 Switches (Cisco 2960 with Cisco IOS Release 15.0(2) lanbasek9 image or comparable)
- 3 PCs (Windows 7, Vista, or XP with terminal emulation program, such as Tera Term)
- Console cables to configure the Cisco IOS devices via the console ports
- Ethernet cables as shown in the topology

Part 1:   Build the Network and Configure Basic Device Settings

In Part 1, you will configure basic settings on the switches and PCs. Refer to the Addressing Table for device names and address information.

Step 1:   Cable the network as shown in the topology.

Step 2:   Initialize and reload the switches.

Step 3:   Configure IP addresses on PC-A, PC-B, and PC-C.

Refer to the Addressing Table for PC address information.

Step 4:   Configure basic settings for each switch.

a.   Disable DNS lookup.

b.   Configure the device names as shown in the topology.

c.   Assign **class** as the privileged EXEC mode password.

d.   Assign **cisco** as the console and VTY password and enable login for console and vty lines.

e.   Configure synchronous logging for console and vty lines.

Step 5:   Configure VLANs on each switch.

a.   Create and name VLANs according to the VLAN Assignments table.

b.   Configure the IP address listed in the Addressing Table for VLAN 99 on both switches.

c.   Configure F0/6 on S1 as an access port and assign it to VLAN 99.

d.   Configure F0/11 on S2 as an access port and assign it to VLAN 10.

e.   Configure F0/18 on S2 as an access port and assign it to VLAN 99.

f.   Issue **show vlan brief** command to verify VLAN and port assignments.

To which VLAN would an unassigned port, such as F0/8 on S2, belong?

Step 6:   Configure basic switch security.

a.   Configure a MOTD banner to warn users that unauthorized access is prohibited.

b.   Encrypt all passwords.

c.   Shut down all unused physical ports.

d.   Disable the basic web service running.

```
S1(config)# no ip http server
S2(config)# no ip http server
```

e.   Copy the running configuration to startup configuration.

Step 6:   Verify connectivity between devices and VLAN information.

a.   From a command prompt on PC-A, ping the management address of S1. Were the pings successful? Why?

_____

_____

b.   From S1, ping the management address of S2. Were the pings successful? Why?

_____

_____

c.   From a command prompt on PC-B, ping the management addresses on S1 and S2 and the IP address of PC-A and PC-C. Were your pings successful? Why?

_____

_____

d.   From a command prompt on PC-C, ping the management addresses on S1 and S2. Were you successful? Why?

_____

_____

Note: It may be necessary to disable the PC firewall to ping between PCs.

Part 2:   Implement VLAN Security on the Switches

Step 1:   Configure trunk ports on S1 and S2.

a.   Configure port F0/1 on S1 as a trunk port.

```
S1(config)# interface f0/1
S1(config-if)# switchport mode trunk
```

b. Configure port F0/1 on S2 as a trunk port.

```
S2(config)# interface f0/1
S2(config-if)# switchport mode trunk
```

c. Verify trunking on S1 and S2. Issue the **show interface trunk** command on both switches.

```
S1# show interface trunk

Port        Mode            Encapsulation  Status       Native vlan
Fa0/1       on              802.1q         trunking     1


Port        Vlans allowed on trunk
Fa0/1       1-4094


Port        Vlans allowed and active in management domain
Fa0/1       1,10,99,999


Port        Vlans in spanning tree forwarding state and not pruned
Fa0/1       1,10,99,999
```

Step 2:   Change the native VLAN for the trunk ports on S1 and S2.

Changing the native VLAN for trunk ports from VLAN 1 to another VLAN is a good practice for security.

a. What is the current native VLAN for the S1 and S2 F0/1 interfaces?

_____

b. Configure the native VLAN on the S1 F0/1 trunk interface to Management&Native VLAN 99.

```
S1# config t
S1(config)# interface f0/1
S1(config-if)# switchport trunk native vlan 99
```

c. Wait a few seconds. You should start receiving error messages on the console session of S1. What does the %CDP-4-NATIVE_VLAN_MISMATCH: message mean?

_____

d. Configure the native VLAN on the S2 F0/1 trunk interface to VLAN 99.

```
S2(config)# interface f0/1
S2(config-if)# switchport trunk native vlan 99
```

e. Verify that the native VLAN is now 99 on both switches. S1 output is shown below.

```
S1# show interface trunk

Port        Mode            Encapsulation  Status       Native vlan
Fa0/1       on              802.1q         trunking     99


Port        Vlans allowed on trunk
Fa0/1       1-4094


Port        Vlans allowed and active in management domain
```

```
Fa0/1        1,10,99,999

Port         Vlans in spanning tree forwarding state and not pruned
Fa0/1        10,999
```

Step 3: Verify that traffic can successfully cross the trunk link.

a. From a command prompt on PC-A, ping the management address of S1. Were the pings successful? Why?

_____

_____

b. From the console session on S1, ping the management address of S2. Were the pings successful? Why?

_____

c. From a command prompt on PC-B, ping the management addresses on S1 and S2 and the IP address of PC-A and PC-C. Were your pings successful? Why?

_____

d. From a command prompt on PC-C, ping the management addresses on S1 and S2 and the IP address of PC-A. Were you successful? Why?

_____

Step 4: Prevent the use of DTP on S1 and S2.

Cisco uses a proprietary protocol known as the Dynamic Trunking Protocol (DTP) on its switches. Some ports automatically negotiate to trunking. A good practice is to turn off negotiation. You can see this default behavior by issuing the following command:

```
S1# show interface f0/1 switchport
Name: Fa0/1
Switchport: Enabled
Administrative Mode: trunk
Operational Mode: trunk
Administrative Trunking Encapsulation: dot1q
Operational Trunking Encapsulation: dot1q
Negotiation of Trunking: On
<Output Omitted>
```

a. Turn off negotiation on S1.

```
S1(config)# interface f0/1
S1(config-if)# switchport nonegotiate
```

b. Turn off negotiation on S2.

```
S2(config)# interface f0/1
S2(config-if)# switchport nonegotiate
```

c. Verify that negotiation is off by issuing the **show interface f0/1 switchport** command on S1 and S2.

```
S1# show interface f0/1 switchport
Name: Fa0/1
Switchport: Enabled
Administrative Mode: trunk
Operational Mode: trunk
Administrative Trunking Encapsulation: dot1q
Operational Trunking Encapsulation: dot1q
Negotiation of Trunking: Off
<Output Omitted>
```

Step 5:   Secure access ports on S1 and S2.

Even though you shut down unused ports on the switches, if a device is connected to one of those ports and the interface is enabled, trunking could occur. In addition, all ports by default are in VLAN 1. A good practice is to put all unused ports in a "black hole" VLAN. In this step, you will disable trunking on all unused ports. You will also assign unused ports to VLAN 999. For the purposes of this lab, only ports 2 through 5 will be configured on both switches.

a. Issue the **show interface f0/2 switchport** command on S1. Notice the administrative mode and state for trunking negotiation.

```
S1# show interface f0/2 switchport
Name: Fa0/2
Switchport: Enabled
Administrative Mode: dynamic auto
Operational Mode: down
Administrative Trunking Encapsulation: dot1q
Negotiation of Trunking: On
<Output Omitted>
```

b. Disable trunking on S1 access ports.

```
S1(config)# interface range f0/2 - 5
S1(config-if-range)# switchport mode access
S1(config-if-range)# switchport access vlan 999
```

c. Disable trunking on S2 access ports.

d. Verify that port F0/2 is set to access on S1.

```
S1# show interface f0/2 switchport
Name: Fa0/2
Switchport: Enabled
Administrative Mode: static access
Operational Mode: down
Administrative Trunking Encapsulation: dot1q
Negotiation of Trunking: Off
Access Mode VLAN: 999 (BlackHole)
Trunking Native Mode VLAN: 1 (default)
Administrative Native VLAN tagging: enabled
Voice VLAN: none
<Output Omitted>
```

e. Verify that VLAN port assignments on both switches are correct. S1 is shown below as an example.

    S1# **show vlan brief**

VLAN	Name	Status	Ports
1	default	active	Fa0/7, Fa0/8, Fa0/9, Fa0/10
			Fa0/11, Fa0/12, Fa0/13, Fa0/14
			Fa0/15, Fa0/16, Fa0/17, Fa0/18
			Fa0/19, Fa0/20, Fa0/21, Fa0/22
			Fa0/23, Fa0/24, Gi0/1, Gi0/2
10	Data	active	
99	Management&Native	active	Fa0/6
999	BlackHole	active	Fa0/2, Fa0/3, Fa0/4, Fa0/5
1002	fddi-default	act/unsup	
1003	token-ring-default	act/unsup	
1004	fddinet-default	act/unsup	
1005	trnet-default	act/unsup	

Restrict VLANs allowed on trunk ports.

By default, all VLANs are allowed to be carried on trunk ports. For security reasons, it is a good practice to only allow specific desired VLANs to cross trunk links on your network.

f. Restrict the trunk port F0/1 on S1 to only allow VLANs 10 and 99.

    S1(config)# **interface f0/1**

    S1(config-if)# **switchport trunk allowed vlan 10,99**

g. Restrict the trunk port F0/1 on S2 to only allow VLANs 10 and 99.

h. Verify the allowed VLANs. Issue a **show interface trunk** command in privileged EXEC mode on both S1 and S2.

    S1# **show interface trunk**

Port	Mode	Encapsulation	Status	Native vlan
Fa0/1	on	802.1q	trunking	99

Port	Vlans allowed on trunk
Fa0/1	10,99

Port	Vlans allowed and active in management domain
Fa0/1	10,99

Port	Vlans in spanning tree forwarding state and not pruned
Fa0/1	10,99

What is the result?

_____

Reflection

What, if any, are the security problems with the default configuration of a Cisco switch?

_____

_____

_____

_____

3.4.1.1 Class Activity – VLAN Plan

Objective

Implement VLANs to segment a small- to medium-sized network.

Scenario

You are designing a VLAN switched network for your small- to medium- sized business.

Your business owns space on two floors of a high-rise building. The following elements need VLAN consideration and access for planning purposes:

- Management

- Finance

- Sales

- Human Resources

- Network administrator

- General visitors to your business location

You have two Cisco 3560-24PS switches.

Use a word processing software program to design your VLAN-switched network scheme.

Section 1 of your design should include the regular names of your departments, suggested VLAN names and numbers, and which switch ports would be assigned to each VLAN.

Section 2 of your design should list how security would be planned for this switched network.

Once your VLAN plan is finished, complete the reflection questions from this activity.

Save your work. Be able to explain and discuss your VLAN design with another group or with the class.

Required Resources

Word processing program

Reflection

1. What criteria did you use for assigning ports to the VLANs?

_____

2. How could these users access your network if the switches were not physically available to general users via direct connection?

_____

3. Could you reduce the number of switch ports assigned for general users if you used another device to connect them to the VLAN network switch? What would be affected?

_____

Chapter 4 — LAN Redundancy

4.0.1.2 Class Activity – Stormy Traffic

Objective

Explain the purpose of the Spanning Tree Protocol (STP) in a switched LAN environment with redundant switch links.

Scenario

It is your first day on the job as a network administrator for a small- to medium-sized business. The previous network administrator left suddenly after a network upgrade took place for the business.

During the upgrade, a new switch was added. Since the upgrade, many employees complain that they are having trouble accessing the Internet and servers on your network. In fact, most of them cannot access the network at all. Your corporate manager asks you to immediately research what could be causing these connectivity problems and delays.

So you take a look at the equipment operating on your network at your main distribution facility in the building. You notice that the network topology seems to be visually correct and that cables have been connected correctly, routers and switches are powered on and operational, and switches are connected together to provide backup or redundancy.

However, one thing you do notice is that all of your switches' status lights are constantly blinking at a very fast pace to the point that they almost appear solid. You think you have found the problem with the connectivity issues your employees are experiencing.

Use the Internet to research STP. As you research, take notes and describe:

- Broadcast storm

- Switching loops

- The purpose of STP

- Variations of STP

Complete the reflection questions that accompany the PDF file for this activity. Save your work and be prepared to share your answers with the class.

Resources

- Internet access to the World Wide Web

Reflection

1. What is a definition of a broadcast storm? How does a broadcast storm develop?

2. What is a definition of a switching loop? What causes a switching loop?

_____

3. How can you mitigate broadcast storms and switching loops caused by introducing redundant switches to your network?

_____

4. What is the IEEE standard for STP and some other STP variations, as mentioned in the hyperlinks provided?

_____

5. In answer to this scenario, what would be your first step (after visually checking your network) to correcting the described network problem?

_____

4.1.2.10 Lab – Building a Switched Network with Redundant Links

Topology

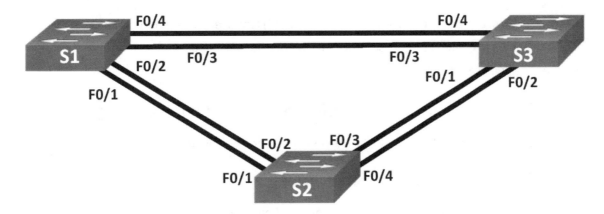

Addressing Table

Device	Interface	IP Address	Subnet Mask
S1	VLAN 1	192.168.1.1	255.255.255.0
S2	VLAN 1	192.168.1.2	255.255.255.0
S3	VLAN 1	192.168.1.3	255.255.255.0

Objectives

Part 1: Build the Network and Configure Basic Device Settings

Part 2: Determine the Root Bridge

Part 3: Observe STP Port Selection Based on Port Cost

Part 4: Observe STP Port Selection Based on Port Priority

Background / Scenario

Redundancy increases the availability of devices in the network topology by protecting the network from a single point of failure. Redundancy in a switched network is accomplished through the use of multiple switches or multiple links between switches. When physical redundancy is introduced into a network design, loops and duplicate frames can occur.

The Spanning Tree Protocol (STP) was developed as a Layer 2 loop-avoidance mechanism for redundant links in a switched network. STP ensures that there is only one logical path between all destinations on the network by intentionally blocking redundant paths that could cause a loop.

In this lab, you will use the **show spanning-tree** command to observe the STP election process of the root bridge. You will also observe the port selection process based on cost and priority.

Note: The switches used are Cisco Catalyst 2960s with Cisco IOS Release 15.0(2) (lanbasek9 image). Other switches and Cisco IOS versions can be used. Depending on the model and Cisco IOS version, the commands available and output produced might vary from what is shown in the labs.

Note: Make sure that the switches have been erased and have no startup configurations. If you are unsure, contact your instructor.

Required Resources

- 3 Switches (Cisco 2960 with Cisco IOS Release 15.0(2) lanbasek9 image or comparable)
- Console cables to configure the Cisco IOS devices via the console ports
- Ethernet cables as shown in the topology

Part 1:   Build the Network and Configure Basic Device Settings

In Part 1, you will set up the network topology and configure basic settings on the switches.

Step 1:   Cable the network as shown in the topology.

Attach the devices as shown in the topology diagram, and cable as necessary.

Step 2:   Initialize and reload the switches as necessary.

Step 3:   Configure basic settings for each switch.

a.   Disable DNS lookup.

b.   Configure the device name as shown in the topology.

c.   Assign **class** as the encrypted privileged EXEC mode password.

d.   Assign **cisco** as the console and vty passwords and enable login for console and vty lines.

e.   Configure logging synchronous for the console line.

f.   Configure a message of the day (MOTD) banner to warn users that unauthorized access is prohibited.

g.   Configure the IP address listed in the Addressing Table for VLAN 1 on all switches.

h.   Copy the running configuration to the startup configuration.

Step 4:   Test connectivity.

Verify that the switches can ping one another.

Can S1 ping S2?   _____

Can S1 ping S3?   _____

Can S2 ping S3?   _____

Troubleshoot until you are able to answer yes to all questions.

Part 2: Determine the Root Bridge

Every spanning-tree instance (switched LAN or broadcast domain) has a switch designated as the root bridge. The root bridge serves as a reference point for all spanning-tree calculations to determine which redundant paths to block.

An election process determines which switch becomes the root bridge. The switch with the lowest bridge identifier (BID) becomes the root bridge. The BID is made up of a bridge priority value, an extended system ID, and the MAC address of the switch. The priority value can range from 0 to 65,535, in increments of 4,096, with a default value of 32,768.

Step 1: Deactivate all ports on the switches.

Step 2: Configure connected ports as trunks.

Step 3: Activate ports F0/2 and F0/4 on all switches.

Step 4: Display spanning tree information.

Issue the **show spanning-tree** command on all three switches. The Bridge ID Priority is calculated by adding the priority value and the extended system ID. The extended system ID is always the VLAN number. In the example below, all three switches have equal Bridge ID Priority values (32769 = 32768 + 1, where default priority = 32768, VLAN number = 1); therefore, the switch with the lowest MAC address becomes the root bridge (S2 in the example).

```
S1# show spanning-tree

VLAN0001
  Spanning tree enabled protocol ieee
  Root ID    Priority    32769
             Address     0cd9.96d2.4000
             Cost        19
             Port        2 (FastEthernet0/2)
             Hello Time   2 sec  Max Age 20 sec  Forward Delay 15 sec

  Bridge ID  Priority    32769  (priority 32768 sys-id-ext 1)
             Address     0cd9.96e8.8a00
             Hello Time   2 sec  Max Age 20 sec  Forward Delay 15 sec
             Aging Time  300 sec

Interface           Role Sts Cost      Prio.Nbr Type
------------------- ---- --- --------- -------- ------------------------------
Fa0/2               Root FWD 19        128.2    P2p
Fa0/4               Altn BLK 19        128.4    P2p


S2# show spanning-tree

VLAN0001
  Spanning tree enabled protocol ieee
  Root ID    Priority    32769
             Address     0cd9.96d2.4000
             This bridge is the root
             Hello Time   2 sec  Max Age 20 sec  Forward Delay 15 sec
```

```
Bridge ID  Priority    32769  (priority 32768 sys-id-ext 1)
           Address     0cd9.96d2.4000
           Hello Time   2 sec  Max Age 20 sec  Forward Delay 15 sec
           Aging Time  300 sec


Interface          Role Sts Cost      Prio.Nbr Type
------------------ ---- --- --------- -------- -------------------------------
Fa0/2              Desg FWD 19         128.2    P2p
Fa0/4              Desg FWD 19         128.4    P2p
```

S3# **show spanning-tree**

```
VLAN0001
  Spanning tree enabled protocol ieee
  Root ID    Priority    32769
             Address     0cd9.96d2.4000
             Cost        19
             Port        2 (FastEthernet0/2)
             Hello Time   2 sec  Max Age 20 sec  Forward Delay 15 sec

  Bridge ID  Priority    32769  (priority 32768 sys-id-ext 1)
             Address     0cd9.96e8.7400
             Hello Time   2 sec  Max Age 20 sec  Forward Delay 15 sec
             Aging Time  300 sec


Interface          Role Sts Cost      Prio.Nbr Type
------------------ ---- --- --------- -------- -------------------------------
Fa0/2              Root FWD 19         128.2    P2p
Fa0/4              Desg FWD 19         128.4    P2p
```

Note: The default STP mode on the 2960 switch is Per VLAN Spanning Tree (PVST).

In the diagram below, record the Role and Status (Sts) of the active ports on each switch in the Topology.

S1 MAC: _____   **S3 MAC:** _____

S1 F0/4: _____   **S3 F0/4:** _____

S1 F0/3: _____   **S3 F0/3:** _____

S1 F0/1:   **S3 F0/2:**

_____

S1 F0/2: _____   **S3 F0/1:** _____

S2 F0/2:   **S2 F0/3:**

_____   _____

S2 F0/1:   **S2 F0/4:**

_____   _____

S2 MAC: _____

Based on the output from your switches, answer the following questions.

Which switch is the root bridge? _____

Why did spanning tree select this switch as the root bridge?

_____

Which ports are the root ports on the switches? _____

Which ports are the designated ports on the switches? _____

What port is showing as an alternate port and is currently being blocked? _____

Why did spanning tree select this port as the non-designated (blocked) port?

_____

_____

_____

_____

Part 3: Observe STP Port Selection Based on Port Cost

The spanning tree algorithm (STA) uses the root bridge as the reference point and then determines which ports to block, based on path cost. The port with the lower path cost is preferred. If port costs are equal, then spanning tree compares BIDs. If the BIDs are equal, then the port priorities are used to break the tie. Lower values are always preferred. In Part 3, you will change the port cost to control which port is blocked by spanning tree.

Step 1: Locate the switch with the blocked port.

With the current configuration, only one switch should have a port that is blocked by STP. Issue the **show spanning-tree** command on both non-root switches. In the example below, spanning tree is blocking port F0/4 on the switch with the highest BID (S1).

```
S1# show spanning-tree


VLAN0001
  Spanning tree enabled protocol ieee
  Root ID    Priority    32769
             Address     0cd9.96d2.4000
             Cost        19
             Port        2 (FastEthernet0/2)
             Hello Time  2 sec  Max Age 20 sec  Forward Delay 15 sec

  Bridge ID  Priority    32769  (priority 32768 sys-id-ext 1)
             Address     0cd9.96e8.8a00
             Hello Time  2 sec  Max Age 20 sec  Forward Delay 15 sec
             Aging Time  300 sec


Interface          Role Sts Cost      Prio.Nbr Type
------------------ ---- --- --------- -------- --------------------------------
Fa0/2              Root FWD 19        128.2    P2p
Fa0/4              Altn BLK 19        128.4    P2p


S3# show spanning-tree


VLAN0001
  Spanning tree enabled protocol ieee
  Root ID    Priority    32769
             Address     0cd9.96d2.4000
             Cost        19
             Port        2 (FastEthernet0/2)
             Hello Time  2 sec  Max Age 20 sec  Forward Delay 15 sec

  Bridge ID  Priority    32769  (priority 32768 sys-id-ext 1)
             Address     0cd9.96e8.7400
             Hello Time  2 sec  Max Age 20 sec  Forward Delay 15 sec
             Aging Time  15  sec


Interface          Role Sts Cost      Prio.Nbr Type
------------------ ---- --- --------- -------- --------------------------------
Fa0/2              Root FWD 19        128.2    P2p
Fa0/4              Desg FWD 19        128.4    P2p
```

Note: Root bridge and port selection may differ in your topology.

Step 2:   Change port cost.

In addition to the blocked port, the only other active port on this switch is the port designated as the root port. Lower the cost of this root port to 18 by issuing the **spanning-tree cost 18** interface configuration mode command.

```
S1(config)# interface f0/2
S1(config-if)# spanning-tree cost 18
```

Step 3:   Observe spanning tree changes.

Re-issue the **show spanning-tree** command on both non-root switches. Observe that the previously blocked port (S1 - F0/4) is now a designated port and spanning tree is now blocking a port on the other non-root switch (S3 - F0/4).

```
S1# show spanning-tree


VLAN0001
  Spanning tree enabled protocol ieee
  Root ID    Priority    32769
             Address     0cd9.96d2.4000
             Cost        18
             Port        2 (FastEthernet0/2)
             Hello Time   2 sec  Max Age 20 sec  Forward Delay 15 sec


  Bridge ID  Priority    32769  (priority 32768 sys-id-ext 1)
             Address     0cd9.96e8.8a00
             Hello Time   2 sec  Max Age 20 sec  Forward Delay 15 sec
             Aging Time  300 sec


Interface          Role Sts Cost      Prio.Nbr Type
------------------ ---- --- --------- -------- --------------------------------

Fa0/2              Root FWD 18        128.2    P2p
Fa0/4              Desg FWD 19        128.4    P2p


S3# show spanning-tree


VLAN0001
  Spanning tree enabled protocol ieee
  Root ID    Priority    32769
             Address     0cd9.96d2.4000
             Cost        19
             Port        2 (FastEthernet0/2)
             Hello Time   2 sec  Max Age 20 sec  Forward Delay 15 sec


  Bridge ID  Priority    32769  (priority 32768 sys-id-ext 1)
             Address     0cd9.96e8.7400
             Hello Time   2 sec  Max Age 20 sec  Forward Delay 15 sec
             Aging Time  300 sec


Interface          Role Sts Cost      Prio.Nbr Type
------------------ ---- --- --------- -------- --------------------------------

Fa0/2              Root FWD 19        128.2    P2p
Fa0/4              Altn BLK 19        128.4    P2p
```

Why did spanning tree change the previously blocked port to a designated port, and block the port that was a designated port on the other switch?

_____

Step 4:   Remove port cost changes.

a. Issue the **no spanning-tree cost 18** interface configuration mode command to remove the cost statement that you created earlier.

```
S1(config)# interface f0/2
S1(config-if)# no spanning-tree cost 18
```

b. Re-issue the **show spanning-tree** command to verify that STP has reset the port on the non-root switches back to the original port settings. It takes approximately 30 seconds for STP to complete the port transition process.

Part 4:   Observe STP Port Selection Based on Port Priority

If port costs are equal, then spanning tree compares BIDs. If the BIDs are equal, then the port priorities are used to break the tie. The default port priority value is 128. STP aggregates the port priority with the port number to break ties. Lower values are always preferred. In Part 4, you will activate redundant paths to each switch to observe how STP selects a port using the port priority.

a. Activate ports F0/1 and F0/3 on all switches.

b. Wait 30 seconds for STP to complete the port transition process, and then issue the **show spanning-tree** command on the non-root switches. Observe that the root port has moved to the lower numbered port linked to the root switch, and blocked the previous root port.

```
S1# show spanning-tree


VLAN0001
  Spanning tree enabled protocol ieee
  Root ID    Priority    32769
             Address     0cd9.96d2.4000
             Cost        19
             Port        1 (FastEthernet0/1)
             Hello Time   2 sec  Max Age 20 sec  Forward Delay 15 sec


  Bridge ID  Priority    32769  (priority 32768 sys-id-ext 1)
             Address     0cd9.96e8.8a00
             Hello Time   2 sec  Max Age 20 sec  Forward Delay 15 sec
             Aging Time  15   sec


  Interface          Role Sts Cost       Prio.Nbr Type
  ------------------ ---- --- --------- -------- --------------------------------
  Fa0/1              Root FWD 19         128.1    P2p
  Fa0/2              Altn BLK 19         128.2    P2p
  Fa0/3              Altn BLK 19         128.3    P2p
  Fa0/4              Altn BLK 19         128.4    P2p


S3# show spanning-tree


VLAN0001
  Spanning tree enabled protocol ieee
```

```
     Root ID    Priority    32769
                Address     0cd9.96d2.4000
                Cost        19
                Port        1 (FastEthernet0/1)
                Hello Time   2 sec  Max Age 20 sec  Forward Delay 15 sec

     Bridge ID  Priority    32769  (priority 32768 sys-id-ext 1)
                Address     0cd9.96e8.7400
                Hello Time   2 sec  Max Age 20 sec  Forward Delay 15 sec
                Aging Time  15  sec

     Interface           Role Sts Cost      Prio.Nbr Type
     ------------------- ---- --- --------- -------- --------------------------------
     Fa0/1               Root FWD 19        128.1    P2p
     Fa0/2               Altn BLK 19        128.2    P2p
     Fa0/3               Desg FWD 19        128.3    P2p
     Fa0/4               Desg FWD 19        128.4    P2p
```

What port did STP select as the root port on each non-root switch? _____

Why did STP select these ports as the root port on these switches?

_____

_____

Reflection

1. After a root bridge has been selected, what is the first value STP uses to determine port selection?

_____

2. If the first value is equal on the two ports, what is the next value that STP uses to determine port selection?

_____

3. If both values are equal on the two ports, what is the next value that STP uses to determine port selection?

_____

4.3.2.3 Lab – Configuring Rapid PVST+, PortFast, and BPDU Guard

Topology

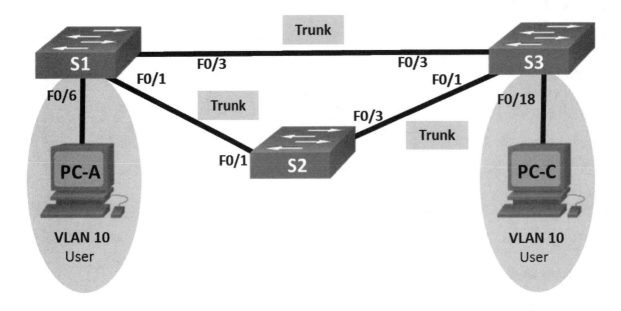

Addressing Table

Device	Interface	IP Address	Subnet Mask
S1	VLAN 99	192.168.1.11	255.255.255.0
S2	VLAN 99	192.168.1.12	255.255.255.0
S3	VLAN 99	192.168.1.13	255.255.255.0
PC-A	NIC	192.168.0.2	255.255.255.0
PC-C	NIC	192.168.0.3	255.255.255.0

VLAN Assignments

VLAN	Name
10	User
99	Management

Objectives

Part 1: Build the Network and Configure Basic Device Settings

Part 2: Configure VLANs, Native VLAN, and Trunks

Part 3: Configure the Root Bridge and Examine PVST+ Convergence

Part 4: Configure Rapid PVST+, PortFast, BPDU Guard, and Examine Convergence

Background / Scenario

The Per-VLAN Spanning Tree (PVST) protocol is Cisco proprietary. Cisco switches default to PVST. Rapid PVST+ (IEEE 802.1w) is an enhanced version of PVST+ and allows for faster spanning-tree calculations and convergence in response to Layer 2 topology changes. Rapid PVST+ defines three port states: discarding, learning, and forwarding, and provides multiple enhancements to optimize network performance.

In this lab, you will configure the primary and secondary root bridge, examine PVST+ convergence, configure Rapid PVST+ and compare its convergence to PVST+. In addition, you will configure edge ports to transition immediately to a forwarding state using PortFast and prevent the edge ports from forwarding BDPUs using BDPU guard.

Note: This lab provides minimal assistance with the actual commands necessary for configuration. However, the required commands are provided in Appendix A. Test your knowledge by trying to configure the devices without referring to the appendix.

Note: The switches used with CCNA hands-on labs are Cisco Catalyst 2960s with Cisco IOS Release 15.0(2) (lanbasek9 image). Other switches and Cisco IOS versions can be used. Depending on the model and Cisco IOS version, the commands available and output produced might vary from what is shown in the labs.

Note: Make sure that the switches have been erased and have no startup configurations. If you are unsure, contact your instructor.

Required Resources

- 3 Switches (Cisco 2960 with Cisco IOS Release 15.0(2) lanbasek9 image or comparable)
- 2 PCs (Windows 7, Vista, or XP with terminal emulation program, such as Tera Term)
- Console cables to configure the Cisco IOS devices via the console ports
- Ethernet cables as shown in the topology

Part 1: Build the Network and Configure Basic Device Settings

In Part 1, you will set up the network topology and configure basic settings, such as the interface IP addresses, device access, and passwords.

Step 1: Cable the network as shown in the topology.

Step 2: Configure PC hosts.

Step 3: Initialize and reload the switches as necessary.

Step 4: Configure basic settings for each switch.

a. Disable DNS lookup.

b. Configure the device name as shown in the Topology.

c. Assign **cisco** as the console and vty passwords and enable login.

d. Assign **class** as the encrypted privileged EXEC mode password.

e. Configure **logging synchronous** to prevent console messages from interrupting command entry.

f. Shut down all switch ports.

g. Copy the running configuration to startup configuration.

Part 2: Configure VLANs, Native VLAN, and Trunks

In Part 2, you will create VLANs, assign switch ports to VLANs, configure trunk ports, and change the native VLAN for all switches.

Note: The required commands for Part 2 are provided in Appendix A. Test your knowledge by trying to configure the VLANs, native VLAN, and trunks without referring to the appendix.

Step 1: Create VLANs.

Use the appropriate commands to create VLANs 10 and 99 on all of the switches. Name VLAN 10 as **User** and VLAN 99 as **Management**.

```
S1(config)# vlan 10
S1(config-vlan)# name User
S1(config-vlan)# vlan 99
S1(config-vlan)# name Management

S2(config)# vlan 10
S2(config-vlan)# name User
S2(config-vlan)# vlan 99
S2(config-vlan)# name Management

S3(config)# vlan 10
S3(config-vlan)# name User
S3(config-vlan)# vlan 99
S3(config-vlan)# name Management
```

Step 2: Enable user ports in access mode and assign VLANs.

For S1 F0/6 and S3 F0/18, enable the ports, configure them as access ports, and assign them to VLAN 10.

Step 3: Configure trunk ports and assign to native VLAN 99.

For ports F0/1 and F0/3 on all switches, enable the ports, configure them as trunk ports, and assign them to native VLAN 99.

Step 4: Configure the management interface on all switches.

Using the Addressing Table, configure the management interface on all switches with the appropriate IP address.

Step 5: Verify configurations and connectivity.

Use the **show vlan brief** command on all switches to verify that all VLANs are registered in the VLAN table and that the correct ports are assigned.

Use the **show interfaces trunk** command on all switches to verify trunk interfaces.

Use the **show running-config** command on all switches to verify all other configurations.

What is the default setting for spanning-tree mode on Cisco switches?

_____

Verify connectivity between PC-A and PC-C. Was your ping successful? _____   .

If your ping was unsuccessful, troubleshoot the configurations until the issue is resolved.

Note: It may be necessary to disable the PC firewall to successfully ping between PCs.

Part 3: Configure the Root Bridge and Examine PVST+ Convergence

In Part 3, you will determine the default root in the network, assign the primary and secondary root, and use the **debug** command to examine convergence of PVST+.

Note: The required commands for Part 3 are provided in Appendix A. Test your knowledge by trying to configure the root bridge without referring to the appendix.

Step 1: Determine the current root bridge.

Which command allows a user to determine the spanning-tree status of a Cisco Catalyst switch for all VLANs? Write the command in the space provided.

_____

Use the command on all three switches to determine the answers to the following questions:

Note: There are three instances of the spanning tree on each switch. The default STP configuration on Cisco switches is PVST+, which creates a separate spanning tree instance for each VLAN (VLAN 1 and any user-configured VLANs).

What is the bridge priority of switch S1 for VLAN 1? _____

What is the bridge priority of switch S2 for VLAN 1? _____

What is the bridge priority of switch S3 for VLAN 1? _____

Which switch is the root bridge? _____

Why was this switch elected as the root bridge?

_____

Step 2: Configure a primary and secondary root bridge for all existing VLANs.

Having a root bridge (switch) elected by MAC address may lead to a suboptimal configuration. In this lab, you will configure switch S2 as the root bridge and S1 as the secondary root bridge.

a. Configure switch S2 to be the primary root bridge for all existing VLANs. Write the command in the space provided.

_____

b. Configure switch S1 to be the secondary root bridge for all existing VLANs. Write the command in the space provided.

_____

Use the **show spanning-tree** command to answer the following questions:

What is the bridge priority of S1 for VLAN 1? _____

What is the bridge priority of S2 for VLAN 1? _____

Which interface in the network is in a blocking state? _____

Step 3: Change the Layer 2 topology and examine convergence.

To examine PVST+ convergence, you will create a Layer 2 topology change while using the **debug** command to monitor spanning-tree events.

a. Enter the **debug spanning-tree events** command in privileged EXEC mode on switch S3.

```
S3# debug spanning-tree events
Spanning Tree event debugging is on
```

b. Create a topology change by disabling interface F0/1 on S3.

```
S3(config)# interface f0/1
S3(config-if)# shutdown
*Mar  1 00:58:56.225: STP: VLAN0001 new root port Fa0/3, cost 38
*Mar  1 00:58:56.225: STP: VLAN0001 Fa0/3 -> listening
*Mar  1 00:58:56.225: STP[1]: Generating TC trap for port FastEthernet0/1
*Mar  1 00:58:56.225: STP: VLAN0010 new root port Fa0/3, cost 38
```

```
*Mar  1 00:58:56.225: STP: VLAN0010 Fa0/3 -> listening
*Mar  1 00:58:56.225: STP[10]: Generating TC trap for port FastEthernet0/1
*Mar  1 00:58:56.225: STP: VLAN0099 new root port Fa0/3, cost 38
*Mar  1 00:58:56.225: STP: VLAN0099 Fa0/3 -> listening
*Mar  1 00:58:56.225: STP[99]: Generating TC trap for port FastEthernet0/1
*Mar  1 00:58:56.242: %LINEPROTO-5-UPDOWN: Line protocol on Interface Vlan1, changed
state to down
*Mar  1 00:58:56.242: %LINEPROTO-5-UPDOWN: Line protocol on Interface Vlan99, changed
state to down
*Mar  1 00:58:58.214: %LINK-5-CHANGED: Interface FastEthernet0/1, changed state to ad-
ministratively down
*Mar  1 00:58:58.230: STP: VLAN0001 sent Topology Change Notice on Fa0/3
*Mar  1 00:58:58.230: STP: VLAN0010 sent Topology Change Notice on Fa0/3
*Mar  1 00:58:58.230: STP: VLAN0099 sent Topology Change Notice on Fa0/3
*Mar  1 00:58:59.220: %LINEPROTO-5-UPDOWN: Line protocol on Interface FastEthernet0/1,
changed state to down
*Mar  1 00:59:11.233: STP: VLAN0001 Fa0/3 -> learning
*Mar  1 00:59:11.233: STP: VLAN0010 Fa0/3 -> learning
*Mar  1 00:59:11.233: STP: VLAN0099 Fa0/3 -> learning
*Mar  1 00:59:26.240: STP[1]: Generating TC trap for port FastEthernet0/3
*Mar  1 00:59:26.240: STP: VLAN0001 Fa0/3 -> forwarding
*Mar  1 00:59:26.240: STP[10]: Generating TC trap for port FastEthernet0/3
*Mar  1 00:59:26.240: STP: VLAN0010 sent Topology Change Notice on Fa0/3
*Mar  1 00:59:26.240: STP: VLAN0010 Fa0/3 -> forwarding
*Mar  1 00:59:26.240: STP[99]: Generating TC trap for port FastEthernet0/3
*Mar  1 00:59:26.240: STP: VLAN0099 Fa0/3 -> forwarding
*Mar  1 00:59:26.248: %LINEPROTO-5-UPDOWN: Line protocol on Interface Vlan1, changed
state to up
*Mar  1 00:59:26.248: %LINEPROTO-5-UPDOWN: Line protocol on Interface Vlan99, changed
state to up
```

Note: Before proceeding, use the **debug** output to verify that all VLANs on F0/3 have reached a forward-ing state then use the command **no debug spanning-tree events** to stop the **debug** output.

Through which port states do each VLAN on F0/3 proceed during network convergence?

_____

_____

Using the time stamp from the first and last STP debug message, calculate the time (to the nearest sec-ond) that it took for the network to converge. **Hint**: The debug timestamp format is date hh.mm.ss:msec.

_____

_____

Part 4: Configure Rapid PVST+, PortFast, BPDU Guard, and Examine Convergence

In Part 4, you will configure Rapid PVST+ on all switches. You will configure PortFast and BPDU guard on all access ports, and then use the **debug** command to examine Rapid PVST+ convergence.

Note: The required commands for Part 4 are provided in Appendix A. Test your knowledge by trying to configure the Rapid PVST+, PortFast, and BPDU guard without referring to the appendix.

Step 1:   Configure Rapid PVST+.

a. Configure S1 for Rapid PVST+. Write the command in the space provided.

_____

b. Configure S2 and S3 for Rapid PVST+.

c. Verify configurations with the **show running-config | include spanning-tree mode** command.

```
S1# show running-config | include spanning-tree mode
spanning-tree mode rapid-pvst

S2# show running-config | include spanning-tree mode
spanning-tree mode rapid-pvst

S3# show running-config | include spanning-tree mode
spanning-tree mode rapid-pvst
```

Step 2:   Configure PortFast and BPDU Guard on access ports.

PortFast is a feature of spanning tree that transitions a port immediately to a forwarding state as soon as it is turned on. This is useful in connecting hosts so that they can start communicating on the VLAN instantly, rather than waiting on spanning tree. To prevent ports that are configured with PortFast from forwarding BPDUs, which could change the spanning tree topology, BPDU guard can be enabled. At the receipt of a BPDU, BPDU guard disables a port configured with PortFast.

a. Configure interface F0/6 on S1 with PortFast. Write the command in the space provided.

_____

b. Configure interface F0/6 on S1 with BPDU guard. Write the command in the space provided.

_____

c. Globally configure all non-trunking ports on switch S3 with PortFast. Write the command in the space provided.

_____

d. Globally configure all non-trunking PortFast ports on switch S3 with BPDU guard. Write the command in the space provided.

_____

Step 3:   Examine Rapid PVST+ convergence.

a. Enter the **debug spanning-tree events** command in privileged EXEC mode on switch S3.

b. Create a topology change by enabling interface F0/1 on switch S3.

```
S3(config)# interface f0/1
S3(config-if)# no shutdown
*Mar  1 01:28:34.946: %LINK-3-UPDOWN: Interface FastEthernet0/1, changed state to up
*Mar  1 01:28:37.588: RSTP(1): initializing port Fa0/1
*Mar  1 01:28:37.588: RSTP(1): Fa0/1 is now designated
```

```
*Mar  1 01:28:37.588: RSTP(10): initializing port Fa0/1
*Mar  1 01:28:37.588: RSTP(10): Fa0/1 is now designated
*Mar  1 01:28:37.588: RSTP(99): initializing port Fa0/1
*Mar  1 01:28:37.588: RSTP(99): Fa0/1 is now designated
*Mar  1 01:28:37.597: RSTP(1): transmitting a proposal on Fa0/1
*Mar  1 01:28:37.597: RSTP(10): transmitting a proposal on Fa0/1
*Mar  1 01:28:37.597: RSTP(99): transmitting a proposal on Fa0/1
*Mar  1 01:28:37.597: RSTP(1): updt roles, received superior bpdu on Fa0/1
*Mar  1 01:28:37.597: RSTP(1): Fa0/1 is now root port
*Mar  1 01:28:37.597: RSTP(1): Fa0/3 blocked by re-root
*Mar  1 01:28:37.597: RSTP(1): synced Fa0/1
*Mar  1 01:28:37.597: RSTP(1): Fa0/3 is now alternate
*Mar  1 01:28:37.597: RSTP(10): updt roles, received superior bpdu on Fa0/1
*Mar  1 01:28:37.597: RSTP(10): Fa0/1 is now root port
*Mar  1 01:28:37.597: RSTP(10): Fa0/3 blocked by re-root
*Mar  1 01:28:37.597: RSTP(10): synced Fa0/1
*Mar  1 01:28:37.597: RSTP(10): Fa0/3 is now alternate
*Mar  1 01:28:37.597: RSTP(99): updt roles, received superior bpdu on Fa0/1
*Mar  1 01:28:37.605: RSTP(99): Fa0/1 is now root port
*Mar  1 01:28:37.605: RSTP(99): Fa0/3 blocked by re-root
*Mar  1 01:28:37.605: RSTP(99): synced Fa0/1
*Mar  1 01:28:37.605: RSTP(99): Fa0/3 is now alternate
*Mar  1 01:28:37.605: STP[1]: Generating TC trap for port FastEthernet0/1
*Mar  1 01:28:37.605: STP[10]: Generating TC trap for port FastEthernet0/1
*Mar  1 01:28:37.605: STP[99]: Generating TC trap for port FastEthernet0/1
*Mar  1 01:28:37.622: RSTP(1): transmitting an agreement on Fa0/1 as a response to a
proposal
*Mar  1 01:28:37.622: RSTP(10): transmitting an agreement on Fa0/1 as a response to a
proposal
*Mar  1 01:28:37.622: RSTP(99): transmitting an agreement on Fa0/1 as a response to a
proposal
*Mar  1 01:28:38.595: %LINEPROTO-5-UPDOWN: Line protocol on Interface FastEthernet0/1,
changed state to up
```

Using the time stamp from the first and last RSTP debug message, calculate the time that it took for the network to converge.

_____

Reflection

1. What is the main benefit of using Rapid PVST+?

_____

2. How does configuring a port with PortFast allow for faster convergence?

_____

3. What protection does BPDU guard provide?

_____

Appendix A – Switch Configuration Commands

Switch S1

```
S1(config)# vlan 10
S1(config-vlan)# name User
S1(config-vlan)# vlan 99
S1(config-vlan)# name Management
S1(config-vlan)# exit
S1(config)# interface f0/6
S1(config-if)# no shutdown
S1(config-if)# switchport mode access
S1(config-if)# switchport access vlan 10
S1(config-if)# interface f0/1
S1(config-if)# no shutdown
S1(config-if)# switchport mode trunk
S1(config-if)# switchport trunk native vlan 99
S1(config-if)# interface f0/3
S1(config-if)# no shutdown
S1(config-if)# switchport mode trunk
S1(config-if)# switchport trunk native vlan 99
S1(config-if)# interface vlan 99
S1(config-if)# ip address 192.168.1.11 255.255.255.0
S1(config-if)# exit
S1(config)# spanning-tree vlan 1,10,99 root secondary
S1(config)# spanning-tree mode rapid-pvst
S1(config)# interface f0/6
S1(config-if)# spanning-tree portfast
S1(config-if)# spanning-tree bpduguard enable
```

Switch S2

```
S2(config)# vlan 10
S2(config-vlan)# name User
S2(config-vlan)# vlan 99
S2(config-vlan)# name Management
S2(config-vlan)# exit
S2(config)# interface f0/1
S2(config-if)# no shutdown
S2(config-if)# switchport mode trunk
S2(config-if)# switchport trunk native vlan 99
S2(config-if)# interface f0/3
S2(config-if)# no shutdown
S2(config-if)# switchport mode trunk
S2(config-if)# switchport trunk native vlan 99
S2(config-if)# interface vlan 99
S2(config-if)# ip address 192.168.1.12 255.255.255.0
S2(config-if)# exit
```

```
S2(config)# spanning-tree vlan 1,10,99 root primary
S2(config)# spanning-tree mode rapid-pvst
```

Switch S3

```
S3(config)# vlan 10
S3(config-vlan)# name User
S3(config-vlan)# vlan 99
S3(config-vlan)# name Management
S3(config-vlan)# exit
S3(config)# interface f0/18
S3(config-if)# no shutdown
S3(config-if)# switchport mode access
S3(config-if)# switchport access vlan 10
S3(config-if)# spanning-tree portfast
S3(config-if)# spanning-tree bpduguard enable
S3(config-if)# interface f0/1
S3(config-if)# no shutdown
S3(config-if)# switchport mode trunk
S3(config-if)# switchport trunk native vlan 99
S3(config-if)# interface f0/3
S3(config-if)# no shutdown
S3(config-if)# switchport mode trunk
S3(config-if)# switchport trunk native vlan 99
S3(config-if)# interface vlan 99
S3(config-if)# ip address 192.168.1.13 255.255.255.0
S3(config-if)# exit
S3(config)# spanning-tree mode rapid-pvst
```

4.4.3.4 Lab – Configuring HSRP and GLBP

Topology

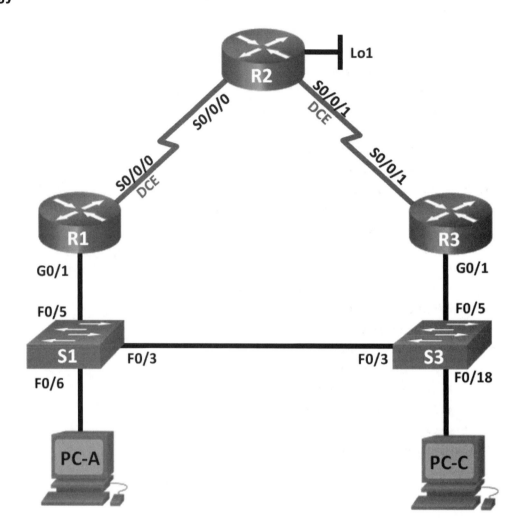

Addressing Table

Device	Interface	IP Address	Subnet Mask	Default Gateway
R1	G0/1	192.168.1.1	255.255.255.0	N/A
	S0/0/0 (DCE)	10.1.1.1	255.255.255.252	N/A
R2	S0/0/0	10.1.1.2	255.255.255.252	N/A
	S0/0/1 (DCE)	10.2.2.2	255.255.255.252	N/A
	Lo1	209.165.200.225	255.255.255.224	N/A
R3	G0/1	192.168.1.3	255.255.255.0	N/A
	S0/0/1	10.2.2.1	255.255.255.252	N/A
S1	VLAN 1	192.168.1.11	255.255.255.0	192.168.1.1
S3	VLAN 1	192.168.1.13	255.255.255.0	192.168.1.3
PC-A	NIC	192.168.1.31	255.255.255.0	192.168.1.1
PC-C	NIC	192.168.1.33	255.255.255.0	192.168.1.3

Objectives

Part 1: Build the Network and Verify Connectivity

Part 2: Configure First Hop Redundancy using HSRP

Part 3: Configure First Hop Redundancy using GLBP

Background / Scenario

Spanning tree provides loop-free redundancy between switches within your LAN. However, it does not provide redundant default gateways for end-user devices within your network if one of your routers fails. First Hop Redundancy Protocols (FHRPs) provide redundant default gateways for end devices with no end-user configuration necessary.

In this lab, you will configure two FHRPs. In Part 2, you will configure Cisco's Hot Standby Routing Protocol (HSRP), and in Part 3 you will configure Cisco's Gateway Load Balancing Protocol (GLBP).

Note: The routers used with CCNA hands-on labs are Cisco 1941 Integrated Services Routers (ISRs) with Cisco IOS Release 15.2(4)M3 (universalk9 image). The switches used are Cisco Catalyst 2960s with Cisco IOS Release 15.0(2) (lanbasek9 image). Other routers, switches, and Cisco IOS versions can be used. Depending on the model and Cisco IOS version, the commands available and output produced might vary from what is shown in the labs. Refer to the Router Interface Summary Table at the end of this lab for the correct interface identifiers.

Note: Make sure that the routers and switches have been erased and have no startup configurations. If you are unsure, contact your instructor.

Required Resources

- 3 Routers (Cisco 1941 with Cisco IOS Release 15.2(4)M3 universal image or comparable)
- 2 Switches (Cisco 2960 with Cisco IOS Release 15.0(2) lanbasek9 image or comparable)
- 2 PCs (Windows 7, Vista, or XP with terminal emulation program, such as Tera Term)
- Console cables to configure the Cisco IOS devices via the console ports
- Ethernet and serial cables as shown in the topology

Part 1: Build the Network and Verify Connectivity

In Part 1, you will set up the network topology and configure basic settings, such as the interface IP addresses, static routing, device access, and passwords.

Step 1: Cable the network as shown in the topology.

Attach the devices as shown in the topology diagram, and cable as necessary.

Step 2: Configure PC hosts.

Step 3: Initialize and reload the routers and switches as necessary.

Step 4: Configure basic settings for each router.

a. Disable DNS lookup.

b. Configure the device name as shown in the topology.

c. Configure IP addresses for the routers as listed in the Addressing Table.

  d. Set clock rate to **128000** for all DCE serial interfaces.

  e. Assign **class** as the encrypted privileged EXEC mode password.

  f. Assign **cisco** for the console and vty password and enable login.

  g. Configure **logging synchronous** to prevent console messages from interrupting command entry.

  h. Copy the running configuration to the startup configuration.

Step 5: Configure basic settings for each switch.

  a. Disable DNS lookup.

  b. Configure the device name as shown in the topology.

  c. Assign **class** as the encrypted privileged EXEC mode password.

  d. Configure IP addresses for the switches as listed in the Addressing Table.

  e. Configure the default gateway on each switch.

  f. Assign **cisco** for the console and vty password and enable login.

  g. Configure **logging synchronous** to prevent console messages from interrupting command entry.

  h. Copy the running configuration to the startup configuration.

Step 6: Verify connectivity between PC-A and PC-C.

Ping from PC-A to PC-C. Were the ping results successful? _____

If the pings are not successful, troubleshoot the basic device configurations before continuing.

Note: It may be necessary to disable the PC firewall to successfully ping between PCs.

Step 7: Configure routing.

  a. Configure EIGRP on the routers and use AS of 1. Add all the networks, except 209.165.200.224/27 into the EIGRP process.

  b. Configure a default route on R2 using Lo1 as the exit interface to 209.165.200.224/27 network and redistribute this route into the EIGRP process.

Step 8: Verify connectivity.

  a. From PC-A, you should be able to ping every interface on R1, R2, R3, and PC-C. Were all pings successful? _____

  b. From PC-C, you should be able to ping every interface on R1, R2, R3, and PC-A. Were all pings successful? _____

Part 2: Configure First Hop Redundancy Using HSRP

Even though the topology has been designed with some redundancy (two routers and two switches on the same LAN network), both PC-A and PC-C are configured with only one gateway address. PC-A is using R1 and PC-C is using R3. If either of these routers or the interfaces on the routers went down, the PC could lose its connection to the Internet.

In Part 2, you will test how the network behaves both before and after configuring HSRP. To do this, you will determine the path that packets take to the loopback address on R2.

Step 1: Determine the path for Internet traffic for PC-A and PC-C.

  a. From a command prompt on PC-A, issue a **tracert** command to the 209.165.200.225 loopback address of R2.

```
C:\ tracert 209.165.200.225
Tracing route to 209.165.200.225 over a maximum of 30 hops

    1    1 ms    1 ms    1 ms  192.168.1.1
    2   13 ms   13 ms   13 ms  209.165.200.225


Trace complete.
```

What path did the packets take from PC-A to 209.165.200.225? _____

b.   From a command prompt on PC-C, issue a **tracert** command to the 209.165.200.225 loopback address of R2.

What path did the packets take from PC-C to 209.165.200.225? _____

Step 2:   Start a ping session on PC-A, and break the connection between S1 and R1.

a.   From a command prompt on PC-A, issue a **ping –t** command to the **209.165.200.225** address on R2. Make sure you leave the command prompt window open.

Note: The pings continue until you press **Ctrl+C**, or until you close the command prompt window.

```
C:\ ping -t 209.165.200.225
Pinging 209.165.200.225 with 32 bytes of data:
Reply from 209.165.200.225: bytes=32 time=9ms TTL=254
Reply from 209.165.200.225: bytes=32 time=9ms TTL=254
Reply from 209.165.200.225: bytes=32 time=9ms TTL=254
Reply from 209.165.200.225: bytes=32 time=9ms TTL=254
Reply from 209.165.200.225: bytes=32 time=9ms TTL=254
Reply from 209.165.200.225: bytes=32 time=9ms TTL=254
Reply from 209.165.200.225: bytes=32 time=9ms TTL=254
Reply from 209.165.200.225: bytes=32 time=9ms TTL=254
Reply from 209.165.200.225: bytes=32 time=9ms TTL=254
Reply from 209.165.200.225: bytes=32 time=9ms TTL=254
Reply from 209.165.200.225: bytes=32 time=9ms TTL=254
Reply from 209.165.200.225: bytes=32 time=9ms TTL=254
Reply from 209.165.200.225: bytes=32 time=9ms TTL=254
<output omitted>
```

b.   As the ping continues, disconnect the Ethernet cable from F0/5 on S1. You can also shut down the S1 F0/5 interface, which creates the same result.

What happened to the ping traffic?

_____

c.   Repeat Steps 2a and 2b on PC-C and S3. Disconnect cable from F0/5 on S3.

What were your results?

_____

d.   Reconnect the Ethernet cables to F0/5 or enable the F0/5 interface on both S1 and S3, respectively. Re-issue pings to 209.165.200.225 from both PC-A and PC-C to make sure connectivity is re-established.

Step 3:   Configure HSRP on R1 and R3.

In this step, you will configure HSRP and change the default gateway address on PC-A, PC-C, S1, and S2 to the virtual IP address for HSRP. R1 becomes the active router via configuration of the HSRP priority command.

a.   Configure HSRP on R1.

```
R1(config)# interface g0/1
R1(config-if)# standby 1 ip 192.168.1.254
R1(config-if)# standby 1 priority 150
R1(config-if)# standby 1 preempt
```

b.   Configure HSRP on R3.

```
R3(config)# interface g0/1
R3(config-if)# standby 1 ip 192.168.1.254
```

c.   Verify HSRP by issuing the **show standby** command on R1 and R3.

```
R1# show standby
GigabitEthernet0/1 - Group 1
  State is Active
    1 state change, last state change 00:02:11
  Virtual IP address is 192.168.1.254
  Active virtual MAC address is 0000.0c07.ac01
    Local virtual MAC address is 0000.0c07.ac01 (v1 default)
  Hello time 3 sec, hold time 10 sec
    Next hello sent in 0.784 secs
  Preemption enabled
  Active router is local
  Standby router is 192.168.1.3, priority 100 (expires in 9.568 sec)
  Priority 150 (configured 150)
  Group name is "hsrp-Gi0/1-1" (default)


R3# show standby
GigabitEthernet0/1 - Group 1
  State is Standby
    4 state changes, last state change 00:02:20
  Virtual IP address is 192.168.1.254
  Active virtual MAC address is 0000.0c07.ac01
    Local virtual MAC address is 0000.0c07.ac01 (v1 default)
  Hello time 3 sec, hold time 10 sec
    Next hello sent in 2.128 secs
  Preemption disabled
  Active router is 192.168.1.1, priority 150 (expires in 10.592 sec)
  Standby router is local
  Priority 100 (default 100)
  Group name is "hsrp-Gi0/1-1" (default)
```

Using the output shown above, answer the following questions:

Which router is the active router? _____

What is the MAC address for the virtual IP address? _____

What is the IP address and priority of the standby router?

_____

_____

d. Use the **show standby brief** command on R1 and R3 to view an HSRP status summary. Sample output is shown below.

```
R1# show standby brief
                     P indicates configured to preempt.
                     |
Interface   Grp  Pri P State   Active       Standby         Virtual IP
Gi0/1       1    150 P Active  local        192.168.1.3     192.168.1.254


R3# show standby brief
                     P indicates configured to preempt.
                     |
Interface   Grp  Pri P State   Active       Standby         Virtual IP
Gi0/1       1    100   Standby 192.168.1.1  local           192.168.1.254
```

e. Change the default gateway address for PC-A, PC-C, S1, and S3. Which address should you use?

_____

Verify the new settings. Issue a ping from both PC-A and PC-C to the loopback address of R2. Are the pings successful? _____

Step 4: Start a ping session on PC-A and break the connection between the switch that is connected to the Active HSRP router (R1).

a. From a command prompt on PC-A, issue a **ping –t** command to the 209.165.200.225 address on R2. Ensure that you leave the command prompt window open.

b. As the ping continues, disconnect the Ethernet cable from F0/5 on S1 or shut down the F0/5 interface.

What happened to the ping traffic?

_____

_____

_____

Step 5: Verify HSRP settings on R1 and R3.

a. Issue the **show standby brief** command on R1 and R3.

Which router is the active router? _____

b. Reconnect the cable between the switch and the router or enable interface F0/5.

c. Disable the HSRP configuration commands on R1 and R3.

```
R1(config)# interface g0/1
R1(config-if)# no standby 1


R3(config)# interface g0/1
R3(config-if)# no standby 1
```

Part 3: Configure First Hop Redundancy Using GLBP

By default, HSRP does NOT do load balancing. The active router always handles all of the traffic, while the standby router sits unused, unless there is a link failure. This is not an efficient use of resources. GLBP provides nonstop path redundancy for IP by sharing protocol and MAC addresses between redundant gateways. GLBP also allows a group of routers to share the load of the default gateway on a LAN. Configuring GLBP is very similar to HSRP. Load balancing can be done in a variety of ways using GLBP. In this lab, you will use the round-robin method.

Step 1:   Configure GLBP on R1 and R3.

a.   Configure GLBP on R1.

```
R1(config)# interface g0/1
R1(config-if)# glbp 1 ip 192.168.1.254
R1(config-if)# glbp 1 preempt
R1(config-if)# glbp 1 priority 150
R1(config-if)# glbp 1 load-balancing round-robin
```

b.   Configure GLBP on R3.

```
R3(config)# interface g0/1
R3(config-if)# glbp 1 ip 192.168.1.254
R3(config-if)# glbp 1 load-balancing round-robin
```

Step 2:   Verify GLBP on R1 and R3.

a.   Issue the **show glbp brief** command on R1 and R3.

```
R1# show glbp brief
Interface   Grp  Fwd Pri State    Address         Active router   Standby router
Gi0/1       1    -   150 Active   192.168.1.254   local           192.168.1.3
Gi0/1       1    1   -   Active   0007.b400.0101  local           -
Gi0/1       1    2   -   Listen   0007.b400.0102  192.168.1.3     -


R3# show glbp brief
Interface   Grp  Fwd Pri State    Address         Active router   Standby router
Gi0/1       1    -   100 Standby  192.168.1.254   192.168.1.1     local
Gi0/1       1    1   -   Listen   0007.b400.0101  192.168.1.1     -
Gi0/1       1    2   -   Active   0007.b400.0102  local           -
```

Step 3:   Generate traffic from PC-A and PC-C to the R2 loopback interface.

a.   From a command prompt on PC-A, ping the 209.165.200.225 address of R2.

```
C:\> ping 209.165.200.225
```

b.   Issue an **arp –a** command on PC-A. Which MAC address is used for the 192.168.1.254 address?

_____

c.   Generate more traffic to the loopback interface of R2. Issue another **arp –a** command. Did the MAC address change for the default gateway address of 192.168.1.254?

_____

As you can see, both R1 and R3 play a role in forwarding traffic to the loopback interface of R2. Neither router remains idle.

Step 4: Start a ping session on PC-A, and break the connection between the switch that is connected to R1.

a. From a command prompt on PC-A, issue a **ping –t** command to the 209.165.200.225 address on R2. Make sure you leave the command prompt window open.

b. As the ping continues, disconnect the Ethernet cable from F0/5 on S1 or shut down the F0/5 interface.

What happened to the ping traffic?

_____

_____

Reflection

1. Why would there be a need for redundancy in a LAN?

_____

_____

2. If you had a choice, which protocol would you implement in your network, HSRP or GLBP? Explain your choice.

_____

_____

Router Interface Summary Table

Router Interface Summary				
Router Model	**Ethernet Interface #1**	**Ethernet Interface #2**	**Serial Interface #1**	**Serial Interface #2**
1800	Fast Ethernet 0/0 (F0/0)	Fast Ethernet 0/1 (F0/1)	Serial 0/0/0 (S0/0/0)	Serial 0/0/1 (S0/0/1)
1900	Gigabit Ethernet 0/0 (G0/0)	Gigabit Ethernet 0/1 (G0/1)	Serial 0/0/0 (S0/0/0)	Serial 0/0/1 (S0/0/1)
2801	Fast Ethernet 0/0 (F0/0)	Fast Ethernet 0/1 (F0/1)	Serial 0/1/0 (S0/1/0)	Serial 0/1/1 (S0/1/1)
2811	Fast Ethernet 0/0 (F0/0)	Fast Ethernet 0/1 (F0/1)	Serial 0/0/0 (S0/0/0)	Serial 0/0/1 (S0/0/1)
2900	Gigabit Ethernet 0/0 (G0/0)	Gigabit Ethernet 0/1 (G0/1)	Serial 0/0/0 (S0/0/0)	Serial 0/0/1 (S0/0/1)

Note: To find out how the router is configured, look at the interfaces to identify the type of router and how many interfaces the router has. There is no way to effectively list all the combinations of configurations for each router class. This table includes identifiers for the possible combinations of Ethernet and Serial interfaces in the device. The table does not include any other type of interface, even though a specific router may contain one. An example of this might be an ISDN BRI interface. The string in parenthesis is the legal abbreviation that can be used in Cisco IOS commands to represent the interface.

4.5.1.1 Class Activity – Documentation Tree

Objective

Identify common STP configuration issues.

Scenario

The employees in your building are having difficulty accessing a web server on the network. You look for the network documentation that the previous network engineer used before he transitioned to a new job; however, you cannot find any network documentation whatsoever.

Therefore, you decide create your own network recordkeeping system. You decide to start at the access layer of your network hierarchy. This is where redundant switches are located, as well as the company servers, printers, and local hosts.

You create a matrix to record your documentation and include access layer switches on the list. You also decide to document switch names, ports in use, cabling connections, and root ports, designated ports, and alternate ports.

For more detailed instructions on how to design your model, use the student PDF that accompanies this activity.

Resources

- Packet Tracer software
- Word processing software

Directions

Step 1:   Create the topology diagram with three redundant switches.

Step 2:   Connect host devices to the switches.

Step 3:   Create the switch documentation matrix.

a.   Name and switch location

b.   General switch description

c.   Model, IOS version, and image name

d.   Switch serial number

e.   MAC address

f.   Ports currently in use

g.   Cable connections

h.   Root ports

i.   Designated ports, status, and cost

j.   Alternate ports, status, and cost

Step 4:   Use show commands to locate Layer 2 switch information.

a.   show version

b.   show cdp neighbors detail

c.   show spanning-tree

Chapter 5 — Link Aggregation

5.0.1.2 Class Activity – Imagine This

Objective

Explain the operation of link aggregation in a switched LAN environment.

Scenario

It is the end of the work day. In your small- to medium-sized business, you are trying to explain to the network engineers about EtherChannel and how it looks when it is physically set up. The network engineers have difficulties envisioning how two switches could possibly be connected via several links that collectively act as one channel or connection. Your company is definitely considering implementing an EtherChannel network.

Therefore, you end the meeting with an assignment for the engineers. To prepare for the next day's meeting, they are to perform some research and bring to the meeting one graphic representation of an EtherChannel network connection. They are tasked with explaining how an EtherChannel network operates to the other engineers.

When researching EtherChannel, a good question to search for is "What does EtherChannel look like?" Prepare a few slides to demonstrate your research that will be presented to the network engineering group. These slides should provide a solid grasp of how EtherChannels are physically created within a network topology. Your goal is to ensure that everyone leaving the next meeting will have a good idea as to why they would consider moving to a network topology using EtherChannel as an option.

Required Resources

- Internet connectivity for research
- Software program for presentation model

Step 1:   Use the Internet to research graphics depicting EtherChannel.

Step 2:   Prepare a three-slide presentation to share with the class.

a. The first slide should show a very short, concise definition of a switch-to-switch EtherChannel.

b. The second slide should show a graphic of how a switch-to-switch EtherChannel physical topology would look if used in a small- to medium-sized business.

c. The third slide should list three advantages of using EtherChannel.

5.2.1.4 Lab – Configuring EtherChannel

Topology

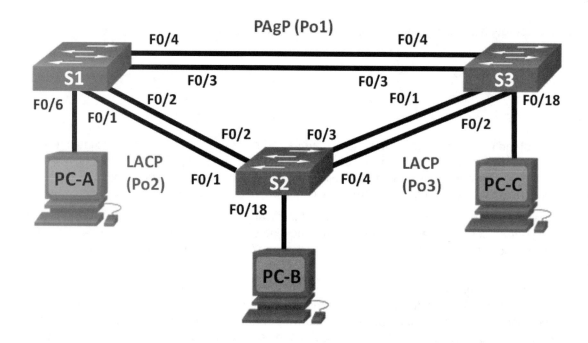

Addressing Table

Device	Interface	IP Address	Subnet Mask
S1	VLAN 99	192.168.99.11	255.255.255.0
S2	VLAN 99	192.168.99.12	255.255.255.0
S3	VLAN 99	192.168.99.13	255.255.255.0
PC-A	NIC	192.168.10.1	255.255.255.0
PC-B	NIC	192.168.10.2	255.255.255.0
PC-C	NIC	192.168.10.3	255.255.255.0

Objectives

Part 1: Configure Basic Switch Settings

Part 2: Configure PAgP

Part 3: Configure LACP

Background / Scenario

Link aggregation allows the creation of logical links that are comprised of two or more physical links. This provides increased throughput beyond using only one physical link. Link aggregation also provides redundancy if one of the links fails.

In this lab, you will configure EtherChannel, a form of link aggregation used in switched networks. You will configure EtherChannel using Port Aggregation Protocol (PAgP) and Link Aggregation Control Protocol (LACP).

Note: PAgP is a Cisco-proprietary protocol that you can only run on Cisco switches and on switches that are licensed vendors to support PAgP. LACP is a link aggregation protocol that is defined by IEEE 802.3ad, and it is not associated with any specific vendor.

LACP allows Cisco switches to manage Ethernet channels between switches that conform to the 802.3ad protocol. You can configure up to 16 ports to form a channel. Eight of the ports are in active mode and the other eight are in standby mode. When any of the active ports fail, a standby port becomes active. Standby mode works only for LACP, not for PAgP.

Note: The switches used with CCNA hands-on labs are Cisco Catalyst 2960s with Cisco IOS Release 15.0(2) (lanbasek9 image). Other switches and Cisco IOS versions can be used. Depending on the model and Cisco IOS version, the commands available and output produced might vary from what is shown in the labs.

Note: Make sure that the switches have been erased and have no startup configurations. If you are unsure, contact your instructor.

Required Resources

- 3 Switches (Cisco 2960 with Cisco IOS Release 15.0(2) lanbasek9 image or comparable)
- 3 PCs (Windows 7, Vista, or XP with terminal emulation program, such as Tera Term)
- Console cables to configure the Cisco IOS devices via the console ports
- Ethernet cables as shown in the topology

Part 1: Configure Basic Switch Settings

In Part 1, you will set up the network topology and configure basic settings, such as the interface IP addresses, device access, and passwords.

Step 1: Cable the network as shown in the topology.

Attach the devices as shown in the topology diagram, and cable as necessary.

Step 2: Initialize and reload the switches.

Step 3: Configure basic settings for each switch.

a. Disable DNS lookup.

b. Configure the device name as displayed in the topology.

c. Encrypt plain text passwords.

d. Create a MOTD banner warning users that unauthorized access is prohibited.

e. Assign **class** as the encrypted privileged EXEC mode password.

f. Assign **cisco** as the console and vty password and enable login.

g. Configure logging synchronous to prevent console message from interrupting command entry.

h. Shut down all switchports except the ports connected to PCs.

i. Configure VLAN 99 and name it **Management**.

j. Configure VLAN 10 and name it **Staff**.

k. Configure the switch ports with attached hosts as access ports in VLAN 10.

l. Assign the IP addresses according to the Addressing Table.

m. Copy the running configuration to startup configuration.

Step 4:   Configure the PCs.

Assign IP addresses to the PCs according to the Addressing Table.

Part 2:   Configure PAgP

PAgP is a Cisco proprietary protocol for link aggregation. In Part 2, a link between S1 and S3 will be configured using PAgP.

Step 1:   Configure PAgP on S1 and S3.

For a link between S1 and S3, configure the ports on S1 with PAgP desirable mode and the ports on S3 with PAgP auto mode. Enable the ports after PAgP modes have been configured.

```
S1(config)# interface range f0/3-4
S1(config-if-range)# channel-group 1 mode desirable
Creating a port-channel interface Port-channel 1

S1(config-if-range)# no shutdown


S3(config)# interface range f0/3-4
S3(config-if-range)# channel-group 1 mode auto
Creating a port-channel interface Port-channel 1


S3(config-if-range)# no shutdown
*Mar  1 00:09:12.792: %LINK-3-UPDOWN: Interface FastEthernet0/3, changed state to up
*Mar  1 00:09:12.792: %LINK-3-UPDOWN: Interface FastEthernet0/4, changed state to up
S3(config-if-range)#
*Mar  1 00:09:15.384: %LINEPROTO-5-UPDOWN: Line protocol on Interface FastEthernet0/3,
changed state to up
*Mar  1 00:09:16.265: %LINEPROTO-5-UPDOWN: Line protocol on Interface FastEthernet0/4,
changed state to up
S3(config-if-range)#
*Mar  1 00:09:16.357: %LINK-3-UPDOWN: Interface Port-channel1, changed state to up
*Mar  1 00:09:17.364: %LINEPROTO-5-UPDOWN: Line protocol on Interface Port-channel1,
changed state to up
*Mar  1 00:09:44.383: %LINEPROTO-5-UPDOWN: Line protocol on Interface Vlan1, changed
state to up
```

Step 2:   Examine the configuration on the ports.

Currently the F0/3, F0/4, and Po1 (Port-channel1) interfaces on both S1 and S3 are in access operational mode with the administrative mode in dynamic auto. Verify the configuration using the **show run interface** *interface-id* and **show interfaces** *interface-id* **switchport** commands, respectively. The example configuration outputs for F0/3 on S1 are as follows:

```
S1# show run interface f0/3
Building configuration...

Current configuration : 103 bytes
!
interface FastEthernet0/3
 channel-group 1 mode desirable
```

```
S1# show interfaces f0/3 switchport
Name: Fa0/3
Switchport: Enabled
Administrative Mode: dynamic auto
Operational Mode: static access (member of bundle Po1)
Administrative Trunking Encapsulation: dot1q
Operational Trunking Encapsulation: native
Negotiation of Trunking: On
Access Mode VLAN: 1 (default)
Trunking Native Mode VLAN: 1 (default)
Administrative Native VLAN tagging: enabled
Voice VLAN: none
Administrative private-vlan host-association: none
Administrative private-vlan mapping: none
Administrative private-vlan trunk native VLAN: none
Administrative private-vlan trunk Native VLAN tagging: enabled
Administrative private-vlan trunk encapsulation: dot1q
Administrative private-vlan trunk normal VLANs: none
Administrative private-vlan trunk associations: none
Administrative private-vlan trunk mappings: none
Operational private-vlan: none
Trunking VLANs Enabled: ALL
Pruning VLANs Enabled: 2-1001
Capture Mode Disabled
Capture VLANs Allowed: ALL

Protected: false
Unknown unicast blocked: disabled
Unknown multicast blocked: disabled
Appliance trust: none
```

Step 3: Verify that the ports have been aggregated.

```
S1# show etherchannel summary
Flags:  D - down         P - bundled in port-channel
        I - stand-alone s - suspended
        H - Hot-standby (LACP only)
        R - Layer3       S - Layer2
        U - in use       f - failed to allocate aggregator

        M - not in use, minimum links not met
        u - unsuitable for bundling
        w - waiting to be aggregated
        d - default port


Number of channel-groups in use: 1
Number of aggregators:           1
```

```
Group   Port-channel   Protocol     Ports
------+-------------+-----------+-------------------------------------------------
1       Po1(SU)        PAgP        Fa0/3(P)    Fa0/4(P)
```

S3# **show etherchannel summary**

```
Flags:  D - down          P - bundled in port-channel
        I - stand-alone   s - suspended
        H - Hot-standby (LACP only)
        R - Layer3        S - Layer2
        U - in use        f - failed to allocate aggregator

        M - not in use, minimum links not met
        u - unsuitable for bundling
        w - waiting to be aggregated
        d - default port


Number of channel-groups in use: 1
Number of aggregators:           1

Group   Port-channel   Protocol     Ports
------+-------------+-----------+-------------------------------------------------
1       Po1(SU)        PAgP        Fa0/3(P)    Fa0/4(P)
```

What do the flags, SU and P, indicate in the Ethernet summary?

_____

_____

Step 4: Configure trunk ports.

After the ports have been aggregated, commands applied at the port channel interface affect all the links that were bundled together. Manually configure the Po1 ports on S1 and S3 as trunk ports and assign them to native VLAN 99.

```
S1(config)# interface port-channel 1
S1(config-if)# switchport mode trunk
S1(config-if)# switchport trunk native vlan 99

S3(config)# interface port-channel 1
S3(config-if)# switchport mode trunk
S3(config-if)# switchport trunk native vlan 99
```

Step 5: Verify that the ports are configured as trunk ports.

a. Issue the **show run interface** *interface-id* commands on S1 and S3. What commands are listed for F0/3 and F0/4 on both switches? Compare the results to the running configuration for the Po1 interface? Record your observation.

_____

_____

b. Issue the **show interfaces trunk** and **show spanning-tree** commands on S1 and S3. What trunk port is listed? What is the native VLAN? What is concluding result from the output?

From the **show spanning-tree** output, what is port cost and port priority for the aggregated link?

Part 3: Configure LACP

LACP is an open source protocol for link aggregation developed by the IEEE. In Part 3, the link between S1 and S2, and the link between S2 and S3 will be configured using LACP. Also, the individual links will be configured as trunks before they are bundled together as EtherChannels.

Step 1: Configure LACP between S1 and S2.

```
S1(config)# interface range f0/1-2
S1(config-if-range)# switchport mode trunk
S1(config-if-range)# switchport trunk native vlan 99
S1(config-if-range)# channel-group 2 mode active
Creating a port-channel interface Port-channel 2

S1(config-if-range)# no shutdown


S2(config)# interface range f0/1-2
S2(config-if-range)# switchport mode trunk
S2(config-if-range)# switchport trunk native vlan 99
S2(config-if-range)# channel-group 2 mode passive
Creating a port-channel interface Port-channel 2

S2(config-if-range)# no shutdown
```

Step 2: Verify that the ports have been aggregated.

What protocol is Po2 using for link aggregation? Which ports are aggregated to form Po2? Record the command used to verify.

Step 3: Configure LACP between S2 and S3.

a. Configure the link between S2 and S3 as Po3 and use LACP as the link aggregation protocol.

```
S2(config)# interface range f0/3-4
S2(config-if-range)# switchport mode trunk
S2(config-if-range)# switchport trunk native vlan 99
S2(config-if-range)# channel-group 3 mode active
```

```
Creating a port-channel interface Port-channel 3
S2(config-if-range)# no shutdown

S3(config)# interface range f0/1-2
S3(config-if-range)# switchport mode trunk
S3(config-if-range)# switchport trunk native vlan 99
S3(config-if-range)# channel-group 3 mode passive
Creating a port-channel interface Port-channel 3

S3(config-if-range)# no shutdown
```

b. Verify that the EtherChannel has formed.

Step 4: Verify end-to-end connectivity.

Verify that all devices can ping each other within the same VLAN. If not, troubleshoot until there is end-to-end connectivity.

Note: It may be necessary to disable the PC firewall to ping between PCs.

Reflection

What could prevent EtherChannels from forming?

_____

5.2.2.4 Lab – Troubleshooting EtherChannel

Topology

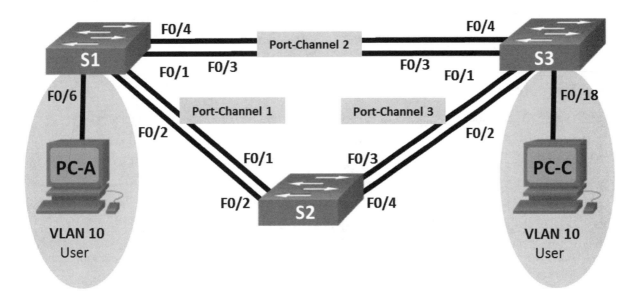

Addressing Table

Device	Interface	IP Address	Subnet Mask
S1	VLAN 99	192.168.1.11	255.255.255.0
S2	VLAN 99	192.168.1.12	255.255.255.0
S3	VLAN 99	192.168.1.13	255.255.255.0
PC-A	NIC	192.168.0.2	255.255.255.0
PC-C	NIC	192.168.0.3	255.255.255.0

VLAN Assignments

VLAN	Name
10	User
99	Management

Objectives

Part 1: Build the Network and Load Device Configurations

Part 2: Troubleshoot EtherChannel

Background / Scenario

The switches at your company were configured by an inexperienced network administrator. Several errors in the configuration have resulted in speed and connectivity issues. Your manager has asked you to troubleshoot and correct the configuration errors and document your work. Using your knowledge of EtherChannel and standard testing methods, find and correct the errors. Ensure that all of the EtherChannels use Port Aggregation Protocol (PAgP), and that all hosts are reachable.

Note: The switches used are Cisco Catalyst 2960s with Cisco IOS Release 15.0(2) (lanbasek9 image). Other switches and Cisco IOS versions can be used. Depending on the model and Cisco IOS version, the commands available and output produced might vary from what is shown in the labs.

Note: Make sure that the switches have been erased and have no startup configurations. If you are unsure, contact your instructor.

Required Resources

- 3 Switches (Cisco 2960 with Cisco IOS Release 15.0(2) lanbasek9 image or comparable)
- 2 PCs (Windows 7, Vista, or XP with a terminal emulation program, such as Tera Term)
- Console cables to configure the Cisco IOS devices via the console ports
- Ethernet cables as shown in the topology

Part 1:   Build the Network and Load Device Configurations

In Part 1, you will set up the network topology, configure basic settings on the PC hosts, and load configurations on the switches.

Step 1:   Cable the network as shown in the topology.

Step 2:   Configure the PC hosts.

Step 3:   Erase the startup and VLAN configurations and reload the switches.

Step 4:   Load switch configurations.

Load the following configurations into the appropriate switch. All switches have the same passwords. The privileged EXEC password is **class**. The password for console and vty access is **cisco**. As all switches are Cisco devices, the network administrator decided to use Cisco's PAgP on all port channels configured with EtherChannel. Switch S2 is the root bridge for all VLANs in the topology.

Switch S1 Configuration:

```
hostname S1
interface range f0/1-24, g0/1-2
shutdown
exit
enable secret class
no ip domain lookup
line vty 0 15
password cisco
login
line con 0
 password cisco
 logging synchronous
 login
 exit
```

```
vlan 10
 name User
vlan 99
 Name Management
interface range f0/1-2
 switchport mode trunk

 channel-group 1 mode active
 switchport trunk native vlan 99
 no shutdown
interface range f0/3-4
 channel-group 2 mode desirable
 switchport trunk native vlan 99

 no shutdown
interface f0/6
 switchport mode access
 switchport access vlan 10
 no shutdown
interface vlan 99
 ip address 192.168.1.11 255.255.255.0
interface port-channel 1
 switchport trunk native vlan 99
 switchport mode trunk
interface port-channel 2
 switchport trunk native vlan 99
 switchport mode access
```

Switch S2 Configuration:

```
hostname S2
interface range f0/1-24, g0/1-2
 shutdown
 exit
enable secret class
no ip domain lookup
line vty 0 15
 password cisco
 login
line con 0
 password cisco
 logging synchronous
 login
 exit
vlan 10
 name User
vlan 99
```

```
 name Management
spanning-tree vlan 1,10,99 root primary
interface range f0/1-2
 switchport mode trunk
 channel-group 1 mode desirable
 switchport trunk native vlan 99
 no shutdown
interface range f0/3-4
 switchport mode trunk
 channel-group 3 mode desirable
 switchport trunk native vlan 99

interface vlan 99
 ip address 192.168.1.12 255.255.255.0
interface port-channel 1
 switchport trunk native vlan 99
 switchport trunk allowed vlan 1,99

interface port-channel 3
 switchport trunk native vlan 99
 switchport trunk allowed vlan 1,10,99
 switchport mode trunk
```

Switch S3 Configuration:

```
hostname S3
interface range f0/1-24, g0/1-2
 shutdown
 exit
enable secret class
no ip domain lookup
line vty 0 15
 password cisco
 login
line con 0
 password cisco
 logging synchronous
 login
 exit
vlan 10
 name User
vlan 99
 name Management
interface range f0/1-2
```

```
interface range f0/3-4
 switchport mode trunk


 channel-group 3 mode desirable
 switchport trunk native vlan 99
 no shutdown
interface f0/18
 switchport mode access
 switchport access vlan 10
 no shutdown
interface vlan 99
 ip address 192.168.1.13 255.255.255.0




interface port-channel 3
 switchport trunk native vlan 99
 switchport mode trunk
```

Step 5: Save your configuration.

Part 2: Troubleshoot EtherChannel

In Part 2, you must examine the configurations on all switches, make corrections if needed, and verify full functionality.

Step 1: Troubleshoot S1.

a. Use the **show interfaces trunk** command to verify that the port channels are functioning as trunk ports.

Do port channels 1 and 2 appear as trunked ports? _____

b. Use the **show etherchannel summary** command to verify that interfaces are configured in the correct port channel, the proper protocol is configured, and the interfaces are in use.

Based on the output, are there any EtherChannel issues? If issues are found, record them in the space provided below.

_____

_____

c. Use the command **show run | begin interface Port-channel** command to view the running configuration beginning with the first port channel interface.

d. Resolve all problems found in the outputs from the previous **show** commands. Record the commands used to correct the configurations.

_____

_____

_____

_____

_____

e. Use the **show interfaces trunk** command to verify trunk settings.

f. Use the **show etherchannel summary** command to verify that the port channels are up and in use.

Step 2: Troubleshoot S2.

a. Issue the command to verify that the port channels are functioning as trunk ports. Record the command used in the space provided below.

_____

Based on the output, are there any issues with the configurations? If issues are found, record them in the space provided below.

_____

_____

b. Issue the command to verify that interfaces are configured in the correct port channel and the proper protocol is configured.

Based on the output, are there any EtherChannel issues? If issues are found, record them in the space provided below.

_____

c. Use the command **show run | begin interface Port-channel** to view the running configuration beginning with the first port-channel interface.

d. Resolve all problems found in the outputs from the previous **show** commands. Record the commands used to correct the configuration.

_____

_____

_____

_____

_____

e. Issue the command to verify trunk settings.

f. Issue the command to verify that the port channels are functioning. Remember that port channel issues can be caused by either end of the link.

Step 3: Troubleshoot S3.

a. Issue the command to verify that the port channels are functioning as trunk ports.

Based on the output, are there any issues with the configurations? If issues are found, record them in the space provided below.

_____

_____

b. Issue the command to verify that the interfaces are configured in the correct port channel and that the proper protocol is configured.

Based on the output, are there any EtherChannel issues? If issues are found, record them in the space provided below.

_____

_____

c. Use the command **show run | begin interface Port-channel** command to view the running configuration beginning with the first port channel interface.

d. Resolve all problems found. Record the commands used to correct the configuration.

_____

_____

_____

_____

_____

_____

_____

e. Issue the command to verify trunk settings. Record the command used in the space provided below.

_____

f. Issue the command to verify that the port channels are functioning. Record the command used in the space provided below.

_____

Step 4: Verify EtherChannel and Connectivity.

a. Use the **show interfaces etherchannel** command to verify full functionality of the port channels.

b. Verify connectivity of the management VLAN.

Can S1 ping S2? _____

Can S1 ping S3? _____

Can S2 ping S3? _____

c. Verify connectivity of PCs.

Can PC-A ping PC-C? _____

If EtherChannels are not fully functional, connectivity between switches does not exist, or connectivity between hosts does not exist. Troubleshoot to resolve any remaining issues.

Note: It may be necessary to disable the PC firewall for pings between the PCs to succeed.

5.3.1.1 Class Activity – Linking Up

Objective

Describe link aggregation.

Scenario

Many bottlenecks occur on your small- to medium-sized business network, even though you have configured VLANs, STP, and other network traffic options on the company's switches.

Instead of keeping the switches as they are currently configured, you would like to try EtherChannel as an option for, at least, part of the network to see if it will lesson traffic congestion between your access and distribution layer switches.

Your company uses Catalyst 3560 switches at the distribution layer and Catalyst 2960 and 2950 switches at the access layer of the network. To verify if these switches can perform EtherChannel, you visit the *System Requirements to Implement EtherChannel on Catalyst Switches*. This site allows you to gather more information to determine if EtherChannel is a good option for the equipment and network currently in place.

After researching the models, you decide to use a simulation software program to practice configuring EtherChannel before implementing it live on your network. As a part of this procedure, you ensure that the equipment simulated in Packet Tracer will support these practice configurations.

Resources

- World Wide Web connectivity
- Packet Tracer software
- Word processing or spreadsheet software

Directions

Step 1:   Visit *System Requirements to Implement EtherChannel on Catalyst Switches***.**

a.   Pay particular attention to the Catalyst 3560, 2960, and 2950 model information.

b.   Record any information you feel would be useful to deciding whether to use EtherChannel in your company.

Step 2:   Create a matrix to record the information you recorded in Step 1b, including:

a.   Number of ports allowed to bundled for an EtherChannel group

b.   Maximum group bandwidth supported by bundling the ports

c.   IOS version needed to support EtherChannel on the switch model

d.   Load balancing availability

e.   Load balancing configuration options

f.   Network layers supported for EtherChannel operation

Step 3:   Open Packet Tracer.

a.   Notice how many ports are available to bundle for EtherChannel on all three switch models.

b.   Check all three models to see how many EtherChannel groups you could create on each model.

c.   Make sure the IOS version is recent enough to support all EtherChannel configurations.

d.   Do not configure your simulated network, but do check the models available in the Packet Tracer to make sure they will support all the EtherChannel configuration options.

Step 4:   Share your matrix with another group or the class.

Chapter 6 — Inter-VLAN Routing

6.0.1.2 Class Activity – Switching to Local-Network Channels

Objective

Configure routing between VLANs in a small to medium-sized business network.

Scenario

You work for a small- to medium-sized business. As the network administrator, you are responsible for ensuring that your network operates efficiently and securely.

Several years ago, you created VLANs on your only switch for two of your departments, Accounting and Sales. As the business has grown, it has become apparent that sometimes these two departments must share company files and network resources.

You discuss this scenario with network administrators in a few branches of your company. They tell you to consider using inter-VLAN routing.

Research the concept of inter-VLAN routing. Design a simple presentation to show your manager how you would use inter-VLAN routing to allow the Accounting and Sales departments to remain separate, but share company files and network resources.

Resources

- Internet connection
- Software presentation program

Directions

Work with a partner to complete this activity.

Step 1:   Use your Internet connection to research how inter-VLANs operate.

a.   Use a search engine to locate a few basic articles, or short videos, that discuss the concept of inter-VLAN routing.

b.   Read the articles, or view the videos, and take notes about how VLANs operate.

c.   Make sure you record where the information was found so that you can include the sources in Step 2 of this activity.

Step 2:   Create a presentation for your manager.

a.   Design a small presentation for your manager listing how you would set up an inter-VLAN routing-based network for your small- to medium-sized business, using no more than five slides.

b.   Include slides which focus on:

1) A synopsis of reasons you would change your current network to an inter-VLAN-switched network. Restate what you are trying to accomplish in your design proposal.

2) A basic, easily understood definition and benefits of using inter-VLAN routing.

       3) A graphic depicting how you would modify your current network to use inter-VLAN routing.

          a)   Your current network utilizes one Cisco 2960 switch and one Cisco 1941 series router.

          b)   Funding for new equipment is not negotiable.

      4) How inter-VLANs could continue to assist with network traffic yet allow departments to communicate with each other.

      5) How inter-VLAN routing would scale for the future.

   c.   Make sure you quote the sources upon which you are basing your presentation.

Step 3:   Present your proposal to the entire class.

6.1.2.4 Lab – Configuring Per-Interface Inter-VLAN Routing

Topology

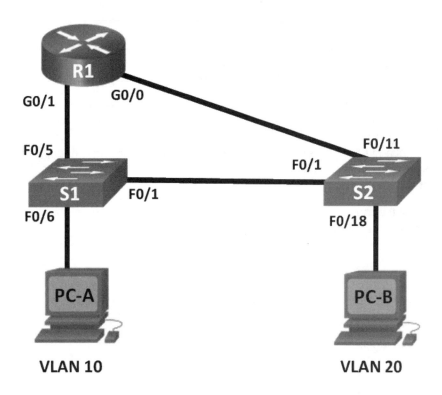

Addressing Table

Device	Interface	IP Address	Subnet Mask	Default Gateway
R1	G0/0	192.168.20.1	255.255.255.0	N/A
	G0/1	192.168.10.1	255.255.255.0	N/A
S1	VLAN 10	192.168.10.11	255.255.255.0	192.168.10.1
S2	VLAN 10	192.168.10.12	255.255.255.0	192.168.10.1
PC-A	NIC	192.168.10.3	255.255.255.0	192.168.10.1
PC-B	NIC	192.168.20.3	255.255.255.0	192.168.20.1

Objectives

Part 1: Build the Network and Configure Basic Device Settings

Part 2: Configure Switches with VLANs and Trunking

Part 3: Verify Trunking, VLANs, Routing, and Connectivity

Background / Scenario

Legacy inter-VLAN routing is seldom used in today's networks; however, it is helpful to configure and understand this type of routing before moving on to router-on-a-stick (trunk-based) inter-VLAN routing or configuring Layer-3 switching. Also, you may encounter per-interface inter-VLAN routing in organizations with very small networks. One of the benefits of legacy inter-VLAN routing is ease of configuration.

In this lab, you will set up one router with two switches attached via the router Gigabit Ethernet interfaces. Two separate VLANs will be configured on the switches, and you will set up routing between the VLANs.

Note: This lab provides minimal assistance with the actual commands necessary to configure the router and switches. The required switch VLAN configuration commands are provided in Appendix A of this lab. Test your knowledge by trying to configure the devices without referring to the appendix.

Note: The routers used with CCNA hands-on labs are Cisco 1941 Integrated Services Routers (ISRs) with Cisco IOS, Release 15.2(4)M3 (universalk9 image). The switches used are Cisco Catalyst 2960s with Cisco IOS, Release 15.0(2) (lanbasek9 image). Other routers, switches and Cisco IOS versions can be used. Depending on the model and Cisco IOS version, the commands available and output produced might vary from what is shown in the labs. Refer to the Router Interface Summary Table at the end of this lab for the correct interface identifiers.

Note: Make sure that the routers and switches have been erased and have no startup configurations. If you are unsure, contact your instructor.

Required Resources

- 1 Router (Cisco 1941 with Cisco IOS Release 15.2(4)M3 universal image or comparable)
- 2 Switches (Cisco 2960 with Cisco IOS Release 15.0(2) lanbasek9 image or comparable)
- 2 PCs (Windows 7, Vista, or XP with terminal emulation program, such as Tera Term)
- Console cables to configure the Cisco IOS devices via the console ports
- Ethernet cables as shown in the topology

Part 1: Build the Network and Configure Basic Device Settings

In Part 1, you will set up the network topology and clear any configurations, if necessary.

Step 1: Cable the network as shown in the topology.

Step 2: Initialize and reload the router and switches.

Step 3: Configure basic settings for R1.

a. Disable DNS lookup.

b. Assign the device name.

c. Assign **class** as the privileged EXEC mode encrypted password.

d. Assign **cisco** as the console and vty line password and enable login.

e. Configure addressing on G0/0 and G0/1 and enable both interfaces.

Step 4: Configure basic settings on S1 and S2.

a. Disable DNS lookup.

b. Assign the device name.

c. Assign **class** as the privileged EXEC mode encrypted password.

d. Assign **cisco** as the console and vty line password and enable login.

Step 5:   Configure basic settings on PC-A and PC-B.

Configure PC-A and PC-B with IP addresses and a default gateway address according to the Addressing Table.

Part 2:   Configure Switches with VLANs and Trunking

In Part 2, you will configure the switches with VLANs and trunking.

Step 1:   Configure VLANs on S1.

a.   On S1, create VLAN 10. Assign **Student** as the VLAN name.

b.   Create VLAN 20. Assign **Faculty-Admin** as the VLAN name.

c.   Configure F0/1 as a trunk port.

d.   Assign ports F0/5 and F0/6 to VLAN 10 and configure both F0/5 and F0/6 as access ports.

e.   Assign an IP address to VLAN 10 and enable it. Refer to the Addressing Table.

f.   Configure the default gateway according to the Addressing Table.

Step 2:   Configure VLANs on S2.

a.   On S2, create VLAN 10. Assign **Student** as the VLAN name.

b.   Create VLAN 20. Assign **Faculty-Admin** as the VLAN name.

c.   Configure F0/1 as a trunk port.

d.   Assign ports F0/11 and F0/18 to VLAN 20 and configure both F0/11 and F0/18 as access ports.

e.   Assign an IP address to VLAN 10 and enable it. Refer to the Addressing Table.

f.   Configure the default gateway according to the Addressing Table.

Part 3:   Verify Trunking, VLANs, Routing, and Connectivity

Step 1:   Verify the R1 routing table.

a.   On R1, issue the **show ip route** command. What routes are listed on R1?

_____

_____

b.   On both S1 and S2, issue the **show interface trunk** command. Is the F0/1 port on both switches set to trunk? _____

c.   Issue a **show vlan brief** command on both S1 and S2. Verify that VLANs 10 and 20 are active and that the proper ports on the switches are in the correct VLANs. Why is F0/1 not listed in any of the active VLANs?

_____

d.   Ping from PC-A in VLAN 10 to PC-B in VLAN 20. If Inter-VLAN routing is functioning correctly, the pings between the 192.168.10.0 network and the 192.168.20.0 should be successful.

   Note: It may be necessary to disable the PC firewall to ping between PCs.

e.   Verify connectivity between devices. You should be able to ping between all devices. Troubleshoot if you are not successful.

Reflection

What is an advantage of using legacy inter-VLAN routing?

_____

_____

_____

Router Interface Summary Table

Router Interface Summary				
Router Model	Ethernet Interface #1	Ethernet Interface #2	Serial Interface #1	Serial Interface #2
1800	Fast Ethernet 0/0 (F0/0)	Fast Ethernet 0/1 (F0/1)	Serial 0/0/0 (S0/0/0)	Serial 0/0/1 (S0/0/1)
1900	Gigabit Ethernet 0/0 (G0/0)	Gigabit Ethernet 0/1 (G0/1)	Serial 0/0/0 (S0/0/0)	Serial 0/0/1 (S0/0/1)
2801	Fast Ethernet 0/0 (F0/0)	Fast Ethernet 0/1 (F0/1)	Serial 0/1/0 (S0/1/0)	Serial 0/1/1 (S0/1/1)
2811	Fast Ethernet 0/0 (F0/0)	Fast Ethernet 0/1 (F0/1)	Serial 0/0/0 (S0/0/0)	Serial 0/0/1 (S0/0/1)
2900	Gigabit Ethernet 0/0 (G0/0)	Gigabit Ethernet 0/1 (G0/1)	Serial 0/0/0 (S0/0/0)	Serial 0/0/1 (S0/0/1)

Note: To find out how the router is configured, look at the interfaces to identify the type of router and how many interfaces the router has. There is no way to effectively list all the combinations of configurations for each router class. This table includes identifiers for the possible combinations of Ethernet and Serial interfaces in the device. The table does not include any other type of interface, even though a specific router may contain one. An example of this might be an ISDN BRI interface. The string in parenthesis is the legal abbreviation that can be used in Cisco IOS commands to represent the interface.

Appendix A: Configuration Commands

Switch S1

```
S1(config)# vlan 10
S1(config-vlan)# name Student
S1(config-vlan)# exit
S1(config)# vlan 20
S1(config-vlan)# name Faculty-Admin
S1(config-vlan)# exit
S1(config)# interface f0/1
S1(config-if)# switchport mode trunk
S1(config-if)# interface range f0/5 - 6
S1(config-if-range)# switchport mode access
S1(config-if-range)# switchport access vlan 10
S1(config-if-range)# interface vlan 10
S1(config-if)# ip address 192.168.10.11 255.255.255.0
S1(config-if)# no shut
S1(config-if)# exit
S1(config)# ip default-gateway 192.168.10.1
```

Switch S2

```
S2(config)# vlan 10
S2(config-vlan)# name Student
S2(config-vlan)# exit
S2(config)# vlan 20
S2(config-vlan)# name Faculty-Admin
S2(config-vlan)# exit
S2(config)# interface f0/1
S2(config-if)# switchport mode trunk
S2(config-if)# interface f0/11
S2(config-if)# switchport mode access
S2(config-if)# switchport access vlan 20
S2(config-if)# interface f0/18
S2(config-if)# switchport mode access
S2(config-if)# switchport access vlan 20
S2(config-if-range)# interface vlan 10
S2(config-if)#ip address 192.168.10.12 255.255.255.0
S2(config-if)# no shut
S2(config-if)# exit
S2(config)# ip default-gateway 192.168.10.1
```

6.1.3.7 Lab – Configuring 802.1Q Trunk-Based Inter-VLAN Routing

Topology

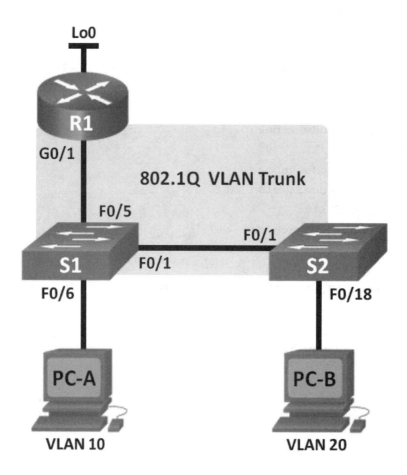

Addressing Table

Device	Interface	IP Address	Subnet Mask	Default Gateway
R1	G0/1.1	192.168.1.1	255.255.255.0	N/A
	G0/1.10	192.168.10.1	255.255.255.0	N/A
	G0/1.20	192.168.20.1	255.255.255.0	N/A
	Lo0	209.165.200.225	255.255.255.224	N/A
S1	VLAN 1	192.168.1.11	255.255.255.0	192.168.1.1
S2	VLAN 1	192.168.1.12	255.255.255.0	192.168.1.1
PC-A	NIC	192.168.10.3	255.255.255.0	192.168.10.1
PC-B	NIC	192.168.20.3	255.255.255.0	192.168.20.1

Switch Port Assignment Specifications

Ports	Assignment	Network
S1 F0/1	802.1Q Trunk	N/A
S2 F0/1	802.1Q Trunk	N/A
S1 F0/5	802.1Q Trunk	N/A
S1 F0/6	VLAN 10 – Students	192.168.10.0/24
S2 F0/18	VLAN 20 – Faculty	192.168.20.0/24

Objectives

Part 1: Build the Network and Configure Basic Device Settings

Part 2: Configure Switches with VLANs and Trunking

Part 3: Configure Trunk-Based Inter-VLAN Routing

Background / Scenario

A second method of providing routing and connectivity for multiple VLANs is through the use of an 802.1Q trunk between one or more switches and a single router interface. This method is also known as router-on-a-stick inter-VLAN routing. In this method, the physical router interface is divided into multiple subinterfaces that provide logical pathways to all VLANs connected.

In this lab, you will configure trunk-based inter-VLAN routing and verify connectivity to hosts on different VLANs as well as with a loopback on the router.

Note: This lab provides minimal assistance with the actual commands necessary to configure trunk-based inter-VLAN routing. However, the required configuration commands are provided in Appendix A of this lab. Test your knowledge by trying to configure the devices without referring to the appendix.

Note: The routers used with CCNA hands-on labs are Cisco 1941 Integrated Services Routers (ISRs) with Cisco IOS, Release 15.2(4)M3 (universalk9 image). The switches used are Cisco Catalyst 2960s with Cisco IOS, Release 15.0(2) (lanbasek9 image). Other routers, switches and Cisco IOS versions can be used. Depending on the model and Cisco IOS version, the commands available and output produced might vary from what is shown in the labs. Refer to the Router Interface Summary Table at the end of the lab for the correct interface identifiers.

Note: Make sure that the routers and switches have been erased and have no startup configurations. If you are unsure, contact your instructor.

Required Resources

- 1 Router (Cisco 1941 with Cisco IOS, release 15.2(4)M3 universal image or comparable)
- 2 Switches (Cisco 2960 with Cisco IOS, release 15.0(2) lanbasek9 image or comparable)
- 2 PCs (Windows 7, Vista, or XP with terminal emulation program, such as Tera Term)
- Console cables to configure the Cisco IOS devices via the console ports
- Ethernet cables as shown in the topology

Part 1: Build the Network and Configure Basic Device Settings

In Part 1, you will set up the network topology and configure basic settings on the PC hosts, switches, and router.

Step 1: Cable the network as shown in the topology.

Step 2: Configure PC hosts.

Step 3: Initialize and reload the router and switches as necessary.

Step 4: Configure basic settings for each switch.

a. Disable DNS lookup.

b. Configure device names as shown in the topology.

    c.   Assign **class** as the privileged EXEC password.

    d.   Assign **cisco** as the console and vty passwords.

    e.   Configure **logging synchronous** for the console line.

    f.   Configure the IP address listed in the Addressing Table for VLAN 1 on both switches.

    g.   Configure the default gateway on both switches.

    h.   Administratively deactivate all unused ports on the switch.

    i.   Copy the running configuration to the startup configuration.

Step 5: Configure basic settings for the router.

    a.   Disable DNS lookup.

    b.   Configure device names as shown in the topology.

    c.   Configure the Lo0 IP address as shown in the Address Table. Do not configure subinterfaces at this time as they will be configured in Part 3.

    d.   Assign **cisco** as the console and vty passwords.

    e.   Assign **class** as the privileged EXEC password.

    f.   Configure **logging synchronous** to prevent console messages from interrupting command entry.

    g.   Copy the running configuration to the startup configuration.

Part 2: Configure Switches with VLANs and Trunking

In Part 2, you will configure the switches with VLANs and trunking.

Note: The required commands for Part 2 are provided in Appendix A. Test your knowledge by trying to configure S1 and S2 without referring to the appendix.

Step 1: Configure VLANs on S1.

    a.   On S1, configure the VLANs and names listed in the Switch Port Assignment Specifications table. Write the commands you used in the space provided.

_____

_____

_____

_____

    b.   On S1, configure the interface connected to R1 as a trunk. Also configure the interface connected to S2 as a trunk. Write the commands you used in the space provided.

_____

_____

    c.   On S1, assign the access port for PC-A to VLAN 10. Write the commands you used in the space provided.

_____

_____

_____

Step 2: Configure VLANs on Switch 2.

a. On S2, configure the VLANs and names listed in the Switch Port Assignment Specifications table.

b. On S2, verify that the VLAN names and numbers match those on S1. Write the command you used in the space provided.

_____

c. On S2, assign the access port for PC-B to VLAN 20.

d. On S2, configure the interface connected to S1 as a trunk.

Part 3: Configure Trunk-Based Inter-VLAN Routing

In Part 3, you will configure R1 to route to multiple VLANs by creating subinterfaces for each VLAN. This method of inter-VLAN routing is called router-on-a-stick.

Note: The required commands for Part 3 are provided in Appendix A. Test your knowledge by trying to configure trunk-based or router-on-a-stick inter-VLAN routing without referring to the appendix.

Step 1: Configure a subinterface for VLAN 1.

a. Create a subinterface on R1 G0/1 for VLAN 1 using 1 as the subinterface ID. Write the command you used in the space provided.

_____

b. Configure the subinterface to operate on VLAN 1. Write the command you used in the space provided.

_____

c. Configure the subinterface with the IP address from the Address Table. Write the command you used in the space provided.

_____

Step 2: Configure a subinterface for VLAN 10.

a. Create a subinterface on R1 G0/1 for VLAN 10 using 10 as the subinterface ID.

b. Configure the subinterface to operate on VLAN 10.

c. Configure the subinterface with the address from the Address Table.

Step 3: Configure a subinterface for VLAN 20.

a. Create a subinterface on R1 G0/1 for VLAN 20 using 20 as the subinterface ID.

b. Configure the subinterface to operate on VLAN 20.

c. Configure the subinterface with the address from the Address Table.

Step 4: Enable the G0/1 interface.

Enable the G0/1 interface. Write the commands you used in the space provided.

_____

Step 5: Verify connectivity.

Enter the command to view the routing table on R1. What networks are listed?

_____

From PC-A, is it possible to ping the default gateway for VLAN 10? _____

From PC-A, is it possible to ping PC-B? _____

From PC-A, is it possible to ping Lo0? _____

From PC-A, is it possible to ping S2? _____

If the answer is **no** to any of these questions, troubleshoot the configurations and correct any errors.

Reflection

What are the advantages of trunk-based or router-on-a-stick inter-VLAN routing?

_____

_____

Router Interface Summary Table

Router Interface Summary				
Router Model	**Ethernet Interface #1**	**Ethernet Interface #2**	**Serial Interface #1**	**Serial Interface #2**
1800	Fast Ethernet 0/0 (F0/0)	Fast Ethernet 0/1 (F0/1)	Serial 0/0/0 (S0/0/0)	Serial 0/0/1 (S0/0/1)
1900	Gigabit Ethernet 0/0 (G0/0)	Gigabit Ethernet 0/1 (G0/1)	Serial 0/0/0 (S0/0/0)	Serial 0/0/1 (S0/0/1)
2801	Fast Ethernet 0/0 (F0/0)	Fast Ethernet 0/1 (F0/1)	Serial 0/1/0 (S0/1/0)	Serial 0/1/1 (S0/1/1)
2811	Fast Ethernet 0/0 (F0/0)	Fast Ethernet 0/1 (F0/1)	Serial 0/0/0 (S0/0/0)	Serial 0/0/1 (S0/0/1)
2900	Gigabit Ethernet 0/0 (G0/0)	Gigabit Ethernet 0/1 (G0/1)	Serial 0/0/0 (S0/0/0)	Serial 0/0/1 (S0/0/1)
Note: To find out how the router is configured, look at the interfaces to identify the type of router and how many interfaces the router has. There is no way to effectively list all the combinations of configurations for each router class. This table includes identifiers for the possible combinations of Ethernet and Serial interfaces in the device. The table does not include any other type of interface, even though a specific router may contain one. An example of this might be an ISDN BRI interface. The string in parenthesis is the legal abbreviation that can be used in Cisco IOS commands to represent the interface.				

Appendix A – Configuration Commands

Switch S1

```
S1(config)# vlan 10
S1(config-vlan)# name Students
S1(config-vlan)# vlan 20
S1(config-vlan)# name Faculty
S1(config-vlan)# exit
```

```
S1(config)# interface f0/1
S1(config-if)# switchport mode trunk
S1(config-if)# interface f0/5
S1(config-if)# switchport mode trunk
S1(config-if)# interface f0/6
S1(config-if)# switchport mode access
S1(config-if)# switchport access vlan 10
```

Switch S2

```
S2(config)# vlan 10
S2(config-vlan)# name Students
S2(config-vlan)# vlan 20
S2(config-vlan)# name Faculty
S2(config)# interface f0/1
S2(config-if)# switchport mode trunk
S2(config-if)# interface f0/18
S2(config-if)# switchport mode access
S2(config-if)# switchport access vlan 20
```

Router R1

```
R1(config)# interface g0/1.1
R1(config-subif)# encapsulation dot1Q 1
R1(config-subif)# ip address 192.168.1.1 255.255.255.0
R1(config-subif)# interface g0/1.10
R1(config-subif)# encapsulation dot1Q 10
R1(config-subif)# ip address 192.168.10.1 255.255.255.0
R1(config-subif)# interface g0/1.20
R1(config-subif)# encapsulation dot1Q 20
R1(config-subif)# ip address 192.168.20.1 255.255.255.0
R1(config-subif)# exit
R1(config)# interface g0/1
R1(config-if)# no shutdown
```

6.3.2.4 Lab – Troubleshooting Inter-VLAN Routing

Topology

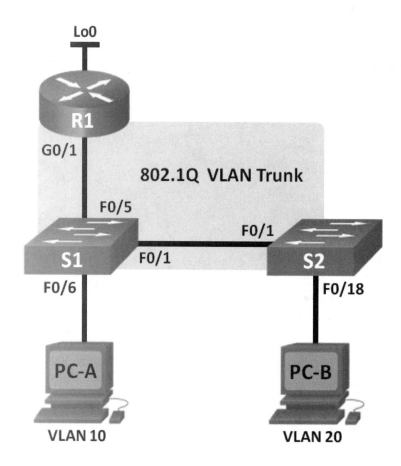

Addressing Table

Device	Interface	IP Address	Subnet Mask	Default Gateway
R1	G0/1.1	192.168.1.1	255.255.255.0	N/A
	G0/1.10	192.168.10.1	255.255.255.0	N/A
	G0/1.20	192.168.20.1	255.255.255.0	N/A
	Lo0	209.165.200.225	255.255.255.224	N/A
S1	VLAN 1	192.168.1.11	255.255.255.0	192.168.1.1
S2	VLAN 1	192.168.1.12	255.255.255.0	192.168.1.1
PC-A	NIC	192.168.10.3	255.255.255.0	192.168.10.1
PC-B	NIC	192.168.20.3	255.255.255.0	192.168.20.1

Switch Port Assignment Specifications

Ports	Assignment	Network
S1 F0/1	802.1Q Trunk	N/A
S2 F0/1	802.1Q Trunk	N/A
S1 F0/5	802.1Q Trunk	N/A
S1 F0/6	VLAN 10 – R&D	192.168.10.0/24
S2 F0/18	VLAN 20 – Engineering	192.168.20.0/24

Objectives

Part 1: Build the Network and Load Device Configurations

Part 2: Troubleshoot the Inter-VLAN Routing Configuration

Part 3: Verify VLAN Configuration, Port Assignment, and Trunking

Part 4: Test Layer 3 Connectivity

Background / Scenario

The network has been designed and configured to support three VLANs. Inter-VLAN routing is provided by an external router using an 802.1Q trunk, also known as router-on-a-stick. Routing to a remote web server, which is simulated by Lo0, is also provided by R1. However, it is not working as designed, and user complaints have not given much insight into the source of the problems.

In this lab, you must first define what is not working as expected, and then analyze the existing configurations to determine and correct the source of the problems. This lab is complete when you can demonstrate IP connectivity between each of the user VLANs and the external web server network, and between the switch management VLAN and the web server network.

Note: The routers used with CCNA hands-on labs are Cisco 1941 Integrated Services Routers (ISRs) with Cisco IOS Release 15.2(4)M3 (universalk9 image). The switches used are Cisco Catalyst 2960s with Cisco IOS Release 15.0(2) (lanbasek9 image). Other routers, switches, and Cisco IOS versions can be used. Depending on the model and Cisco IOS version, the commands available and output produced might vary from what is shown in the labs. Refer to the Router Interface Summary Table at the end of this lab for the correct interface identifiers.

Note: Make sure that the routers and switches have been erased and have no startup configurations. If you are unsure, contact your instructor.

Required Resources

- 1 Router (Cisco 1941 with Cisco IOS Release 15.2(4)M3 universal image or comparable)
- 2 Switches (Cisco 2960 with Cisco IOS Release 15.0(2) lanbasek9 image or comparable)
- 2 PCs (Windows 7, Vista, or XP with terminal emulation program, such as Tera Term)
- Console cables to configure the Cisco IOS devices via the console ports
- Ethernet cables as shown in the topology

Part 1: Build the Network and Load Device Configurations

In Part 1, you will set up the network topology and configure basic settings on the PC hosts, switches, and router.

Step 1: Cable the network as shown in the topology.

Step 2: Configure PC hosts.

Refer to the Addressing Table for PC host address information.

Step 3:   Load router and switch configurations.

Load the following configurations into the appropriate router or switch. All devices have the same passwords; the enable password is **class**, and the line password is **cisco**.

Router R1 Configuration:

```
hostname R1
enable secret class
no ip domain lookup
line con 0
 password cisco
 login
 logging synchronous
line vty 0 4
 password cisco
 login
interface loopback0
 ip address 209.165.200.225 255.255.255.224
interface gigabitEthernet0/1
 no ip address

interface gigabitEthernet0/1.1
 encapsulation dot1q 11

 ip address 192.168.1.1 255.255.255.0
interface gigabitEthernet0/1.10
 encapsulation dot1q 10
 ip address 192.168.11.1 255.255.255.0

interface gigabitEthernet0/1.20
 encapsulation dot1q 20
 ip address 192.168.20.1 255.255.255.0
end
```

Switch S1 Configuration:

```
hostname S1
enable secret class
no ip domain-lookup
line con 0
 password cisco
 login
 logging synchronous
line vty 0 15
 password cisco
 login
vlan 10
 name R&D
 exit
```

```
interface fastethernet0/1
 switchport mode access

interface fastethernet0/5
 switchport mode trunk




interface vlan1
 ip address 192.168.1.11 255.255.255.0
ip default-gateway 192.168.1.1
end
```

Switch S2 Configuration:

```
hostname S2
enable secret class
no ip domain-lookup
line con 0
 password cisco
 login
 logging synchronous
line vty 0 15
 password cisco
 login




vlan 20
 name Engineering
 exit
interface fastethernet0/1
 switchport mode trunk
interface fastethernet0/18
 switchport access vlan 10
 switchport mode access

interface vlan1
 ip address 192.168.1.12 255.255.255.0
ip default-gateway 192.168.1.1
end
```

Step 4:   Save the running configuration to the startup configuration.

Part 2:   Troubleshoot the Inter-VLAN Routing Configuration

In Part 2, you will verify the inter-VLAN routing configuration.

a.   On R1, enter the **show ip route** command to view the routing table.

Which networks are listed?

_____

Are there any networks missing in the routing table? If so, which networks?

_____

What is one possible reason that a route would be missing from the routing table?

_____

b.   On R1, issue the **show ip interface brief** command.

Based on the output, are there any interface issues on the router? If so, what commands would resolve the issues?

_____

_____

_____

c.   On R1, re-issue the **show ip route** command.

Verify that all networks are available in the routing table. If not, continue to troubleshoot until all networks are present.

Part 3:   Verify VLAN Configuration, Port Assignment, and Trunking

In Part 3, you will verify that the correct VLANs exist on both S1 and S2 and that trunking is configured correctly.

Step 1:   Verify VLAN configuration and port assignments.

a.   On S1, enter the **show vlan brief** command to view the VLAN database.

Which VLANs are listed? Ignore VLANs 1002 to 1005.

_____

Are there any VLANs numbers or names missing in the output? If so, list them.

_____

Are the access ports assigned to the correct VLANs? If not, list the missing or incorrect assignments.

_____

If required, what commands would resolve the VLAN issues?

_____

_____

_____

b. On S1, re-issue the **show vlan brief** command to verify configuration.

c. On S2, enter the **show vlan brief** command to view the VLAN database.

Which VLANs are listed? Ignore VLANs 1002 to 1005.

_____

Are there any VLANs numbers or names missing in the output? If so, list them.

_____

Are the access ports assigned to the correct VLANs? If not, list the missing or incorrect assignments.

_____

If required, what commands would resolve the VLAN issues?

_____

_____

_____

d. On S2, re-issue the **show vlan brief** command to verify any configuration changes.

Step 2: Verify trunking interfaces.

a. On S1, enter the **show interface trunk** command to view the trunking interfaces.

Which ports are in trunking mode?

_____

Are there any ports missing in the output? If so, list them.

_____

If required, what commands would resolve the port trunking issues?

_____

_____

b. On S1, re-issue the **show interface trunk** command to verify any configuration changes.

c. On S2, enter the **show interface trunk** command to view the trunking interfaces.

Which ports are in trunking mode?

_____

Are there any ports missing in the output? If so, list them.

_____

If required, what commands would resolve the port trunking issues?

_____

_____

Part 4: Test Layer 3 Connectivity

a. Now that you have corrected multiple configuration issues, let's test connectivity.

From PC-A, is it possible to ping the default gateway for VLAN 10? _____

From PC-A, is it possible to ping PC-B? _____

From PC-A, is it possible to ping Lo0? _____

If the answer is **no** to any of these questions, troubleshoot the configurations and correct the error.

Note: It may be necessary to disable the PC firewall for pings between PCs to be successful.

From PC-A, is it possible to ping S1? _____

From PC-A, is it possible to ping S2? _____

List some of the issues that could still be preventing successful pings to the switches.

_____

_____

b. One way to help resolve where the error is occurring is to do a **tracert** from PC-A to S1.

```
C:\Users\User1> tracert 192.168.1.11
Tracing route to 192.168.1.11 over a maximum of 30 hops
    1    <1 ms    <1 ms    <1 ms   192.168.10.1
    2     *        *        *       Request timed out.
    3     *        *        *       Request timed out.
<output omitted>
```

This output shows that the request from PC-A is reaching the default gateway on R1 g0/1.10, but the packet stops at the router.

c. You have already verified the routing table entries for R1, now execute the **show run | section interface** command to verify VLAN configuration. List any configuration errors.

_____

_____

What commands would resolve any issues found?

_____

_____

_____

d. Verify that that pings from PC-A now reach both S1 and S2.

From PC-A, is it possible to ping S1? _____

From PC-A, is it possible to ping S2? _____

Reflection

What are the advantages of viewing the routing table for troubleshooting purposes?

_____

_____

Router Interface Summary Table

Router Interface Summary				
Router Model	Ethernet Interface #1	Ethernet Interface #2	Serial Interface #1	Serial Interface #2
1800	Fast Ethernet 0/0 (F0/0)	Fast Ethernet 0/1 (F0/1)	Serial 0/0/0 (S0/0/0)	Serial 0/0/1 (S0/0/1)
1900	Gigabit Ethernet 0/0 (G0/0)	Gigabit Ethernet 0/1 (G0/1)	Serial 0/0/0 (S0/0/0)	Serial 0/0/1 (S0/0/1)
2801	Fast Ethernet 0/0 (F0/0)	Fast Ethernet 0/1 (F0/1)	Serial 0/1/0 (S0/1/0)	Serial 0/1/1 (S0/1/1)
2811	Fast Ethernet 0/0 (F0/0)	Fast Ethernet 0/1 (F0/1)	Serial 0/0/0 (S0/0/0)	Serial 0/0/1 (S0/0/1)
2900	Gigabit Ethernet 0/0 (G0/0)	Gigabit Ethernet 0/1 (G0/1)	Serial 0/0/0 (S0/0/0)	Serial 0/0/1 (S0/0/1)
Note: To find out how the router is configured, look at the interfaces to identify the type of router and how many interfaces the router has. There is no way to effectively list all the combinations of configurations for each router class. This table includes identifiers for the possible combinations of Ethernet and Serial interfaces in the device. The table does not include any other type of interface, even though a specific router may contain one. An example of this might be an ISDN BRI interface. The string in parenthesis is the legal abbreviation that can be used in Cisco IOS commands to represent the interface.				

6.4.1.1 Class Activity – The Inside Track

Objective

Explain how Layer 3 switches forward data in a small- to medium-sized business LAN.

Scenario

Your company has just purchased a three-level building. You are the network administrator and must design the company inter-VLAN routing network scheme to serve a few employees on each floor.

Floor 1 is occupied by the HR Department, Floor 2 is occupied by the IT Department, and Floor 3 is occupied by the Sales Department. All Departments must be able to communicate with each other, but at the same time have their own separate working networks.

You brought three Cisco 2960 switches and a Cisco 1941 series router from the old office location to serve network connectivity in the new building. New equipment is non-negotiable.

Refer to the PDF for this activity for further instructions.

Resources

- Software presentation program

Directions

Work with a partner to complete this activity.

Step 1: Design your topology.

a. Use one 2960 switch per floor of your new building.

b. Assign one department to each switch.

c. Pick one of the switches to connect to the 1941 series router.

Step 2: Plan the VLAN scheme.

a. Devise VLAN names and numbers for the HR, IT, and Sales Departments.

b. Include a management VLAN, possibly named Management or Native, numbered to your choosing.

c. Use either IPv4 or v6 as your addressing scheme for the LANs. If using IPv4, you must also use VLSM.

Step 3: Design a graphic to show your VLAN design and address scheme.

Step 4: Choose your inter-VLAN routing method.

a. Legacy (per interface)

b. Router-on-a-Stick

c. Multilayer switching

Step 5: Create a presentation justifying your inter-VLAN routing method of choice.

a. No more than eight slides can be created for the presentation.

b. Present your group's design to the class or to your instructor.

1) Be able to explain the method you chose. What makes it different or more desirable to your business than the other two methods?

2) Be able to show how data moves throughout your network. Verbally explain how the networks are able to communicate using your inter-VLAN method of choice.

Chapter 7 — DHCP

7.0.1.1 Class Activity – Own or Lease?

Objective

Configure DHCP for IPv4 on a LAN switch.

Scenario

This chapter presents the concept of using the DHCP process in a small- to medium-sized business network. This modeling activity describes how very basic wireless ISR devices work using the DHCP process.

Visit http://ui.linksys.com/WRT54GL/4.30.0/Setup.htm, which is a web-based simulator that helps you learn to configure DHCP using a Linksys wireless 54GL router. To the right of the simulator (in the blue description column), you can click **More** to read information about configuring DHCP settings on this particular integrated services router (ISR) simulator.

Practice configuring the ISR's:

- Hostname

- Local IP address with subnet mask

- DHCP (enable and disable)

- Starting IP address

- Maximum number of users to receive an IP DHCP address

- Lease time

- Time zone (use yours or a favorite as an alternative)

When you have completed configuring the settings as listed for this assignment, take a screen shot of your settings by using the **PrtScr** key command. Copy and place your screen shot into a word processing document. Save it and be prepared to discuss your configuration choices with the class.

Required Resources

Internet connectivity

Reflection

1. Why would any network administrator need to save a bank of IP addresses for DHCP **not** to use?

_____

2. You are designing your small- to medium-sized network and you have a choice as to whether to buy a small, generic ISR for DHCP purposes, or use a DHCP full server. Before you read this chapter, how would you make your decision?

_____

7.1.2.4 Lab - Configuring Basic DHCPv4 on a Router

Topology

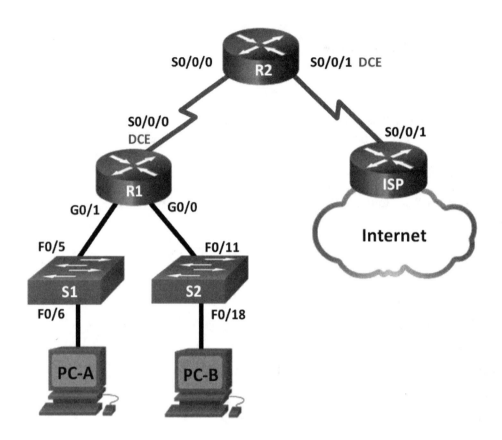

Addressing Table

Device	Interface	IP Address	Subnet Mask	Default Gateway
R1	G0/0	192.168.0.1	255.255.255.0	N/A
	G0/1	192.168.1.1	255.255.255.0	N/A
	S0/0/0 (DCE)	192.168.2.253	255.255.255.252	N/A
R2	S0/0/0	192.168.2.254	255.255.255.252	N/A
	S0/0/1 (DCE)	209.165.200.226	255.255.255.224	N/A
ISP	S0/0/1	209.165.200.225	255.255.255.224	N/A
PC-A	NIC	DHCP	DHCP	DHCP
PC-B	NIC	DHCP	DHCP	DHCP

Objectives

Part 1: Build the Network and Configure Basic Device Settings

Part 2: Configure a DHCPv4 Server and a DHCP Relay Agent

Background / Scenario

The Dynamic Host Configuration Protocol (DHCP) is a network protocol that lets network administrators manage and automate the assignment of IP addresses. Without DHCP, the administrator must manually assign and configure IP addresses, preferred DNS servers, and default gateways. As the network grows in size, this becomes an administrative problem when devices are moved from one internal network to another.

In this scenario, the company has grown in size, and the network administrators can no longer assign IP addresses to devices manually. Your job is to configure the R2 router to assign IPv4 addresses on two different subnets connected to router R1.

Note: This lab provides minimal assistance with the actual commands necessary to configure DHCP. However, the required commands are provided in Appendix A. Test your knowledge by trying to configure the devices without referring to the appendix.

Note: The routers used with CCNA hands-on labs are Cisco 1941 Integrated Services Routers (ISRs) with Cisco IOS Release 15.2(4)M3 (universalk9 image). The switches used are Cisco Catalyst 2960s with Cisco IOS Release 15.0(2) (lanbasek9 image). Other routers, switches and Cisco IOS versions can be used. Depending on the model and Cisco IOS version, the commands available and output produced might vary from what is shown in the labs. Refer to the Router Interface Summary Table at the end of this lab for the correct interface identifiers.

Note: Make sure that the routers and switches have been erased and have no startup configurations. If you are unsure, contact your instructor.

Required Resources

- 3 Routers (Cisco 1941 with Cisco IOS Release 15.2(4)M3 universal image or comparable)
- 2 Switches (Cisco 2960 with Cisco IOS Release 15.0(2) lanbasek9 image or comparable)
- 2 PCs (Windows 7, Vista, or XP with terminal emulation program, such as Tera Term)
- Console cables to configure the Cisco IOS devices via the console ports
- Ethernet and serial cables as shown in the topology

Part 1:   Build the Network and Configure Basic Device Settings

In Part 1, you will set up the network topology and configure the routers and switches with basic settings, such as passwords and IP addresses. You will also configure the IP settings for the PCs in the topology.

Step 1:   Cable the network as shown in the topology.

Step 2:   Initialize and reload the routers and switches.

Step 3:   Configure basic settings for each router.

a. Disable DNS lookup.

b. Configure the device name as shown in the topology.

c. Assign **class** as the encrypted privileged EXEC mode password.

d. Assign **cisco** as the console and vty passwords.

e. Configure **logging synchronous** to prevent console messages from interrupting command entry.

f. Configure the IP addresses for all the router interfaces according to the Addressing Table.

g. Configure the serial DCE interface on R1 and R2 with a clock rate of 128000.

h. Configure EIGRP for R1.

```
R1(config)# router eigrp 1
R1(config-router)# network 192.168.0.0 0.0.0.255
R1(config-router)# network 192.168.1.0 0.0.0.255
R1(config-router)# network 192.168.2.252 0.0.0.3
R1(config-router)# no auto-summary
```

i. Configure EIGRP and a default route to the ISP on R2.

```
R2(config)# router eigrp 1
R2(config-router)# network 192.168.2.252 0.0.0.3
R2(config-router)# redistribute static
R2(config-router)# exit
R2(config)# ip route 0.0.0.0 0.0.0.0 209.165.200.225
```

j. Configure a summary static route on ISP to reach the networks on the R1 and R2 routers.

```
ISP(config)# ip route 192.168.0.0 255.255.252.0 209.165.200.226
```

k. Copy the running configuration to the startup configuration.

Step 4:   Verify network connectivity between the routers.

If any pings between routers fail, correct the errors before proceeding to the next step. Use **show ip route** and **show ip interface brief** to locate possible issues.

Step 5:   Verify the host PCs are configured for DHCP.

Part 2:   Configure a DHCPv4 Server and a DHCP Relay Agent

To automatically assign address information on the network, you will configure R2 as a DHCPv4 server and R1 as a DHCP relay agent.

Step 1:   Configure DHCPv4 server settings on router R2.

On R2, you will configure a DHCP address pool for each of the R1 LANs. Use the pool name **R1G0** for the G0/0 LAN and **R1G1** for the G0/1 LAN. You will also configure the addresses to be excluded from the address pools. Best practice dictates that excluded addresses be configured first, to guarantee that they are not accidentally leased to other devices.

Exclude the first 9 addresses in each R1 LAN starting with .1. All other addresses should be available in the DHCP address pool. Make sure that each DHCP address pool includes a default gateway, the domain **ccna-lab.com**, a DNS server (209.165.200.225), and a lease time of 2 days.

On the lines below, write the commands necessary for configuring DHCP services on router R2, including the DHCP-excluded addresses and the DHCP address pools.

Note: The required commands for Part 2 are provided in Appendix A. Test your knowledge by trying to configure DHCP on R1 and R2 without referring to the appendix.

_____

_____

_____

_____

_____

_____

_____

_____

_____

_____

_____

_____

_____

_____

_____

On PC-A or PC-B, open a command prompt and enter the **ipconfig /all** command. Did either of the host PCs receive an IP address from the DHCP server? Why?

_____

Step 2:   Configure R1 as a DHCP relay agent.

Configure IP helper addresses on R1 to forward all DHCP requests to the R2 DHCP server.

On the lines below, write the commands necessary to configure R1 as a DHCP relay agent for the R1 LANs.

_____

_____

_____

Step 3:   Record IP settings for PC-A and PC-B.

On PC-A and PC-B, issue the **ipconfig /all** command to verify that the PCs have received IP address information from the DHCP server on R2. Record the IP and MAC address for each PC.

_____

Based on the DHCP pool that was configured on R2, what are the first available IP addresses that PC-A and PC-B can lease?

_____

Step 4:   Verify DHCP services and address leases on R2.

    a.   On R2, enter the **show ip dhcp binding** command to view DHCP address leases.

        Along with the IP addresses that were leased, what other piece of useful client identification information is in the output?

        _____

    b.   On R2, enter the **show ip dhcp server statistics** command to view the DHCP pool statistics and message activity.

        How many types of DHCP messages are listed in the output?

        _____

    c.   On R2, enter the **show ip dhcp pool** command to view the DHCP pool settings.

        In the output of the **show ip dhcp pool** command, what does the Current index refer to?

        _____

    d.   On R2, enter the **show run | section dhcp** command to view the DHCP configuration in the running configuration.

    e.   On R1, enter the **show run interface** command for interfaces G0/0 and G0/1 to view the DHCP relay configuration in the running configuration.

Reflection

What do you think is the benefit of using DHCP relay agents instead of multiple routers acting as DHCP servers?

_____

_____

_____

_____

Router Interface Summary Table

Router Interface Summary				
Router Model	**Ethernet Interface #1**	**Ethernet Interface #2**	**Serial Interface #1**	**Serial Interface #2**
1800	Fast Ethernet 0/0 (F0/0)	Fast Ethernet 0/1 (F0/1)	Serial 0/0/0 (S0/0/0)	Serial 0/0/1 (S0/0/1)
1900	Gigabit Ethernet 0/0 (G0/0)	Gigabit Ethernet 0/1 (G0/1)	Serial 0/0/0 (S0/0/0)	Serial 0/0/1 (S0/0/1)
2801	Fast Ethernet 0/0 (F0/0)	Fast Ethernet 0/1 (F0/1)	Serial 0/1/0 (S0/1/0)	Serial 0/1/1 (S0/1/1)
2811	Fast Ethernet 0/0 (F0/0)	Fast Ethernet 0/1 (F0/1)	Serial 0/0/0 (S0/0/0)	Serial 0/0/1 (S0/0/1)
2900	Gigabit Ethernet 0/0 (G0/0)	Gigabit Ethernet 0/1 (G0/1)	Serial 0/0/0 (S0/0/0)	Serial 0/0/1 (S0/0/1)

Note: To find out how the router is configured, look at the interfaces to identify the type of router and how many interfaces the router has. There is no way to effectively list all the combinations of configurations for each router class. This table includes identifiers for the possible combinations of Ethernet and Serial interfaces in the device. The table does not include any other type of interface, even though a specific router may contain one. An example of this might be an ISDN BRI interface. The string in parenthesis is the legal abbreviation that can be used in Cisco IOS commands to represent the interface.

Appendix A – DHCP Configuration Commands

Router R1

```
R1(config)# interface g0/0
R1(config-if)# ip helper-address 192.168.2.254
R1(config-if)# exit
R1(config-if)# interface g0/1
R1(config-if)# ip helper-address 192.168.2.254
```

Router R2

```
R2(config)# ip dhcp excluded-address 192.168.0.1 192.168.0.9
R2(config)# ip dhcp excluded-address 192.168.1.1 192.168.1.9
R2(config)# ip dhcp pool R1G1
R2(dhcp-config)# network 192.168.1.0 255.255.255.0
R2(dhcp-config)# default-router 192.168.1.1
R2(dhcp-config)# dns-server 209.165.200.225
R2(dhcp-config)# domain-name ccna-lab.com
R2(dhcp-config)# lease 2
R2(dhcp-config)# exit
R2(config)# ip dhcp pool R1G0
R2(dhcp-config)# network 192.168.0.0 255.255.255.0
R2(dhcp-config)# default-router 192.168.0.1
R2(dhcp-config)# dns-server 209.165.200.225
R2(dhcp-config)# domain-name ccna-lab.com
R2(dhcp-config)# lease 2
```

7.1.2.5 Lab – Configuring Basic DHCPv4 on a Switch

Topology

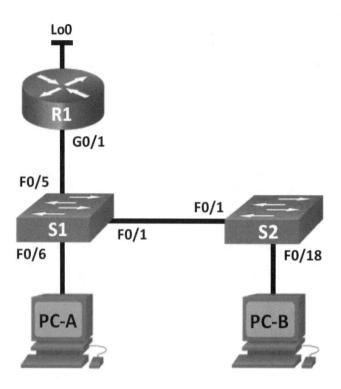

Addressing Table

Device	Interface	IP Address	Subnet Mask
R1	G0/1	192.168.1.10	255.255.255.0
	Lo0	209.165.200.225	255.255.255.224
S1	VLAN 1	192.168.1.1	255.255.255.0
	VLAN 2	192.168.2.1	255.255.255.0

Objectives

Part 1: Build the Network and Configure Basic Device Settings

Part 2: Change the SDM Preference

- Set the SDM preference to lanbase-routing on S1.

Part 3: Configure DHCPv4

- Configure DHCPv4 for VLAN 1.
- Verify DHCPv4 and connectivity.

Part 4: Configure DHCP for Multiple VLANs

- Assign ports to VLAN 2.
- Configure DHCPv4 for VLAN 2.
- Verify DHCPv4 and connectivity.

Part 5: Enable IP Routing

- Enable IP routing on the switch.
- Create static routes.

Background / Scenario

A Cisco 2960 switch can function as a DHCPv4 server. The Cisco DHCPv4 server assigns and manages IPv4 addresses from identified address pools that are associated with specific VLANs and switch virtual interfaces (SVIs). The Cisco 2960 switch can also function as a Layer 3 device and route between VLANs and a limited number of static routes. In this lab, you will configure DHCPv4 for both single and multiple VLANs on a Cisco 2960 switch, enable routing on the switch to allow for communication between VLANs, and add static routes to allow for communication between all hosts.

Note: This lab provides minimal assistance with the actual commands necessary to configure DHCP. However, the required commands are provided in Appendix A. Test your knowledge by trying to configure the devices without referring to the appendix.

Note: The routers used with CCNA hands-on labs are Cisco 1941 Integrated Services Routers (ISRs) with Cisco IOS Release 15.2(4)M3 (universalk9 image). The switches used are Cisco Catalyst 2960s with Cisco IOS Release 15.0(2) (lanbasek9 image). Other routers, switches and Cisco IOS versions can be used. Depending on the model and Cisco IOS version, the commands available and output produced might vary from what is shown in the labs. Refer to the Router Interface Summary Table at the end of this lab for the correct interface identifiers.

Note: Make sure that the router and switches have been erased and have no startup configurations. If you are unsure, contact your instructor.

Required Resources

- 1 Router (Cisco 1941 with Cisco IOS Release 15.2(4)M3 universal image or comparable)
- 2 Switches (Cisco 2960 with Cisco IOS Release 15.0(2) lanbasek9 image or comparable)
- 2 PCs (Windows 7, Vista, or XP with terminal emulation program, such as Tera Term)
- Console cables to configure the Cisco IOS devices via the console ports
- Ethernet cables as shown in the topology

Part 1: Build the Network and Configure Basic Device Settings

Step 1: Cable the network as shown in the topology.

Step 2: Initialize and reload the router and switches.

Step 3: Configure basic setting on devices.

a. Assign device names as shown in the topology.

b. Disable DNS lookup.

c. Assign **class** as the enable password and assign **cisco** as the console and vty passwords.

d. Configure the IP addresses on R1 G0/1 and Lo0 interfaces, according to the Addressing Table.

e. Configure the IP addresses on S1 VLAN 1 and VLAN 2 interfaces, according to the Addressing Table.

f. Save the running configuration to the startup configuration file.

Part 2: Change the SDM Preference

The Cisco Switch Database Manager (SDM) provides multiple templates for the Cisco 2960 switch. The templates can be enabled to support specific roles depending on how the switch is used in the network. In this lab, the sdm lanbase-routing template is enabled to allow the switch to route between VLANs and to support static routing.

Step 1:   Display the SDM preference on S1.

On S1, issue the **show sdm prefer** command in privileged EXEC mode. If the template has not been changed from the factory default, it should still be the **default** template. The **default** template does not support static routing. If IPv6 addressing has been enabled, the template will be **dual-ipv4-and-ipv6 default**.

```
S1# show sdm prefer
The current template is "default" template.
The selected template optimizes the resources in
the switch to support this level of features for
0 routed interfaces and 255 VLANs.

    number of unicast mac addresses:             8K
    number of IPv4 IGMP groups:                  0.25K
    number of IPv4/MAC qos aces:                 0.125k
    number of IPv4/MAC security aces:            0.375k
```

What is the current template?

_____

Step 2:   Change the SDM Preference on S1.

a. Set the SDM preference to **lanbase-routing**. (If lanbase-routing is the current template, please proceed to Part 3.) From global configuration mode, issue the **sdm prefer lanbase-routing** command.

```
S1(config)# sdm prefer lanbase-routing
Changes to the running SDM preferences have been stored, but cannot take effect
until the next reload.
Use 'show sdm prefer' to see what SDM preference is currently active.
```

Which template will be available after reload? _____

b. The switch must be reloaded for the template to be enabled.

```
S1# reload
```

```
System configuration has been modified. Save? [yes/no]: no
Proceed with reload? [confirm]
```

Note: The new template will be used after reboot even if the running configuration has not been saved. To save the running configuration, answer **yes** to save the modified system configuration.

Step 3:   Verify that lanbase-routing template is loaded.

Issue the **show sdm prefer** command to verify that the lanbase-routing template has been loaded on S1.

```
S1# show sdm prefer
 The current template is "lanbase-routing" template.
 The selected template optimizes the resources in
 the switch to support this level of features for
 0 routed interfaces and 255 VLANs.
```

```
number of unicast mac addresses:                    4K
number of IPv4 IGMP groups + multicast routes:      0.25K
number of IPv4 unicast routes:                      0.75K
   number of directly-connected IPv4 hosts:         0.75K
   number of indirect IPv4 routes:                  16
number of IPv6 multicast groups:                    0.375k
number of directly-connected IPv6 addresses:        0.75K
   number of indirect IPv6 unicast routes:          16
number of IPv4 policy based routing aces:           0
number of IPv4/MAC qos aces:                        0.125k
number of IPv4/MAC security aces:                   0.375k
number of IPv6 policy based routing aces:           0
number of IPv6 qos aces:                            0.375k
number of IPv6 security aces:                       127
```

Part 3: Configure DHCPv4

In Part 3, you will configure DHCPv4 for VLAN 1, check IP settings on host computers to validate DHCP functionality, and verify connectivity for all devices in VLAN 1.

Step 1: Configure DHCP for VLAN 1.

a. Exclude the first 10 valid host addresses from network 192.168.1.0/24. Write the command you used in the space provided.

b. Create a DHCP pool named **DHCP1**. Write the command you used in the space provided.

c. Assign the network 192.168.1.0/24 for available addresses. Write the command you used in the space provided.

d. Assign the default gateway as 192.168.1.1. Write the command you used in the space provided.

e. Assign the DNS server as 192.168.1.9. Write the command you used in the space provided.

f. Assign a lease time of 3 days. Write the command you used in the space provided.

g. Save the running configuration to the startup configuration file.

Step 2:   Verify DHCP and connectivity.

a.   On PC-A and PC-B, open the command prompt and issue the **ipconfig** command. If IP information is not present, or if it is incomplete, issue the **ipconfig /release** command, followed by the **ipconfig /renew** command.

For PC-A, list the following:

IP Address: _____

Subnet Mask: _____

Default Gateway: _____

For PC-B, list the following:

IP Address: _____

Subnet Mask: _____

Default Gateway: _____

b.   Test connectivity by pinging from PC-A to the default gateway, PC-B, and R1.

From PC-A, is it possible to ping the VLAN 1 default gateway? _____

From PC-A, is it possible to ping PC-B? _____

From PC-A, is it possible to ping R1 G0/1? _____

If the answer is no to any of these questions, troubleshoot the configurations and correct the error.

Part 4:   Configure DHCPv4 for Multiple VLANs

In Part 4, you will assign PC-A to a port accessing VLAN 2, configure DHCPv4 for VLAN 2, renew the IP configuration of PC-A to validate DHCPv4, and verify connectivity within the VLAN.

Step 1:   Assign a port to VLAN 2.

Place port F0/6 into VLAN 2. Write the command you used in the space provided.

_____

_____

Step 2:   Configure DHCPv4 for VLAN 2

a.   Exclude the first 10 valid host addresses from network 192.168.2.0. Write the command you used in the space provided.

_____

b.   Create a DHCP pool named **DHCP2**. Write the command you used in the space provided.

_____

c.   Assign the network 192.168.2.0/24 for available addresses. Write the command you used in the space provided.

_____

d.   Assign the default gateway as 192.168.2.1. Write the command you used in the space provided.

_____

e.   Assign the DNS server as 192.168.2.9. Write the command you used in the space provided.

_____

f.   Assign a lease time of 3 days. Write the command you used in the space provided.

_____

g.   Save the running configuration to the startup configuration file.

Step 3:   Verify DHCPv4 and connectivity.

a.   On PC-A, open the command prompt and issue the **ipconfig /release** command, followed by **ipconfig /renew** command.

For PC-A, list the following:

IP Address: _____

Subnet Mask: _____

Default Gateway: _____

b.   Test connectivity by pinging from PC-A to the VLAN 2 default gateway and PC-B.

From PC-A, is it possible to ping the default gateway? _____

From PC-A, is it possible to ping PC-B? _____

Were these pings successful? Why?

_____

_____

c.   Issue the **show ip route** command on S1.

What was the result of this command?

_____

_____

Part 5:   Enable IP Routing

In Part 5, you will enable IP routing on the switch, which will allow for inter-VLAN communication. For all networks to communicate, static routes on S1 and R1 must be implemented.

Step 1:   Enable IP routing on S1.

a.   From global configuration mode, use the **ip routing** command to enable routing on S1.

```
S1(config)# ip routing
```

b.   Verify inter-VLAN connectivity.

From PC-A, is it possible to ping PC-B? _____

What function is the switch performing?

_____

c.   View the routing table information for S1.

What route information is contained in the output of this command?

_____

_____

d.   View the routing table information for R1.

What route information is contained in the output of this command?

_____

_____

e.   From PC-A, is it possible to ping R1? _____

From PC-A, is it possible to ping Lo0? _____

Consider the routing table of the two devices, what must be added to communicate between all networks?

_____

Step 2:   Assign static routes.

Enabling IP routing allows the switch to route between VLANs assigned on the switch. For all VLANs to communicate with the router, static routes must be added to the routing table of both the switch and the router.

a.   On S1, create a default static route to R1. Write the command you used in the space provided.

_____

b.   On R1, create a static route to VLAN 2. Write the command you used in the space provided.

_____

c.   View the routing table information for S1.

How is the default static route represented?

_____

d.   View the routing table information for R1.

How is the static route represented?

_____

e.   From PC-A, is it possible to ping R1? _____

From PC-A, is it possible to ping Lo0? _____

Reflection

1. In configuring DHCPv4, why would you exclude the static addresses prior to setting up the DHCPv4 pool?

_____

_____

2. If multiple DHCPv4 pools are present, how does the switch assign the IP information to hosts?

_____

3. Besides switching, what functions can the Cisco 2960 switch perform?

_____

Router Interface Summary Table

Router Interface Summary				
Router Model	**Ethernet Interface #1**	**Ethernet Interface #2**	**Serial Interface #1**	**Serial Interface #2**
1800	Fast Ethernet 0/0 (F0/0)	Fast Ethernet 0/1 (F0/1)	Serial 0/0/0 (S0/0/0)	Serial 0/0/1 (S0/0/1)
1900	Gigabit Ethernet 0/0 (G0/0)	Gigabit Ethernet 0/1 (G0/1)	Serial 0/0/0 (S0/0/0)	Serial 0/0/1 (S0/0/1)
2801	Fast Ethernet 0/0 (F0/0)	Fast Ethernet 0/1 (F0/1)	Serial 0/1/0 (S0/1/0)	Serial 0/1/1 (S0/1/1)
2811	Fast Ethernet 0/0 (F0/0)	Fast Ethernet 0/1 (F0/1)	Serial 0/0/0 (S0/0/0)	Serial 0/0/1 (S0/0/1)
2900	Gigabit Ethernet 0/0 (G0/0)	Gigabit Ethernet 0/1 (G0/1)	Serial 0/0/0 (S0/0/0)	Serial 0/0/1 (S0/0/1)
Note: To find out how the router is configured, look at the interfaces to identify the type of router and how many interfaces the router has. There is no way to effectively list all the combinations of configurations for each router class. This table includes identifiers for the possible combinations of Ethernet and Serial interfaces in the device. The table does not include any other type of interface, even though a specific router may contain one. An example of this might be an ISDN BRI interface. The string in parenthesis is the legal abbreviation that can be used in Cisco IOS commands to represent the interface.				

Appendix A: Configuration Commands

Configure DHCPv4

```
S1(config)# ip dhcp excluded-address 192.168.1.1 192.168.1.10
S1(config)# ip dhcp pool DHCP1
S1(dhcp-config)# network 192.168.1.0 255.255.255.0
S1(dhcp-config)# default-router 192.168.1.1
S1(dhcp-config)# dns-server 192.168.1.9
S1(dhcp-config)# lease 3
```

Configure DHCPv4 for Multiple VLANs

```
S1(config)# interface f0/6
S1(config-if)# switchport access vlan 2
S1(config)# ip dhcp excluded-address 192.168.2.1 192.168.2.10
S1(config)# ip dhcp pool DHCP2
S1(dhcp-config)# network 192.168.2.0 255.255.255.0
S1(dhcp-config)# default-router 192.168.2.1
S1(dhcp-config)# dns-server 192.168.2.9
S1(dhcp-config)# lease 3
```

Enable IP Routing

```
S1(config)# ip routing
S1(config)# ip route 0.0.0.0 0.0.0.0 192.168.1.10
R1(config)# ip route 192.168.2.0 255.255.255.0 g0/1
```

7.1.4.4 Lab – Troubleshooting DHCPv4

Topology

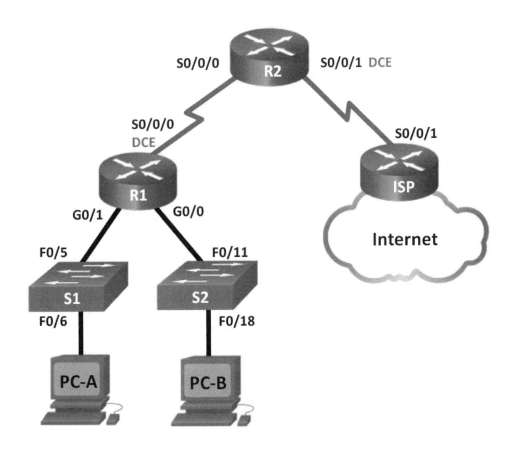

Addressing Table

Device	Interface	IP Address	Subnet Mask	Default Gateway
R1	G0/0	192.168.0.1	255.255.255.128	N/A
	G0/1	192.168.1.1	255.255.255.0	N/A
	S0/0/0 (DCE)	192.168.0.253	255.255.255.252	N/A
R2	S0/0/0	192.168.0.254	255.255.255.252	N/A
	S0/0/1 (DCE)	209.165.200.226	255.255.255.252	N/A
ISP	S0/0/1	209.165.200.225	255.255.255.252	N/A
S1	VLAN 1	192.168.1.2	255.255.255.0	192.168.1.1
S2	VLAN 1	192.168.0.2	255.255.255.128	192.168.0.1
PC-A	NIC	DHCP	DHCP	DHCP
PC-B	NIC	DHCP	DHCP	DHCP

Objectives

Part 1: Build the Network and Configure Basic Device Settings

Part 2: Troubleshoot DHCPv4 Issues

Background / Scenario

The Dynamic Host Configuration Protocol (DHCP) is a network protocol that lets the network administrators manage and automate the assignment of IP addresses. Without DHCP, the administrator must manually assign and configure IP addresses, preferred DNS servers, and the default gateway. As the network grows in size, this becomes an administrative problem when devices are moved from one internal network to another.

In this scenario, the company has grown in size, and the network administrators can no longer assign IP addresses to devices manually. The R2 router has been configured as a DHCP server to assign IP addresses to the host devices on router R1 LANs. Several errors in the configuration have resulted in connectivity issues. You are asked to troubleshoot and correct the configuration errors and document your work.

Ensure that the network supports the following:

    1) The router R2 should function as the DHCP server for the 192.168.0.0/25 and 192.168.1.0/24 networks connected to R1.

    2) All PCs connected to S1 and S2 should receive an IP address in the correct network via DHCP.

Note: The routers used with CCNA hands-on labs are Cisco 1941 Integrated Services Routers (ISRs) with Cisco IOS Release 15.2(4)M3 (universalk9 image). The switches used are Cisco Catalyst 2960s with Cisco IOS Release 15.0(2) (lanbasek9 image). Other routers, switches and Cisco IOS versions can be used. Depending on the model and Cisco IOS version, the commands available and output produced might vary from what is shown in the labs. Refer to the Router Interface Summary Table at the end of this lab for the correct interface identifiers.

Note: Make sure that the routers and switches have been erased and have no startup configurations. If you are unsure, contact your instructor.

Required Resources

- 3 Routers (Cisco 1941 with Cisco IOS Release 15.2(4)M3 universal image or comparable)
- 2 Switches (Cisco 2960 with Cisco IOS Release 15.0(2) lanbasek9 image or comparable)
- 2 PCs (Windows 7, Vista, or XP with terminal emulation program, such as Tera Term)
- Console cables to configure the Cisco IOS devices via the console ports
- Ethernet and serial cables as shown in the topology

Part 1: Build the Network and Configure Basic Device Settings

In Part 1, you will set up the network topology and configure the routers and switches with basic settings, such as passwords and IP addresses. You will also configure the IP settings for the PCs in the topology.

Step 1: Cable the network as shown in the topology.

Step 2: Initialize and reload the routers and switches.

Step 3: Configure basic settings for each router.

    a. Disable DNS lookup.

    b. Configure device name as shown in the topology.

    c. Assign **class** as the privileged EXEC password.

    d. Assign **cisco** as the console and vty passwords.

    e. Configure **logging synchronous** to prevent console messages from interrupting command entry.

f. Configure the IP addresses for all the router interfaces.

g. Set clock rate to **128000** for all DCE router interfaces.

h. Configure EIGRP for R1.

```
R1(config)# router eigrp 1
R1(config-router)# network 192.168.0.0 0.0.0.127
R1(config-router)# network 192.168.0.252 0.0.0.3
R1(config-router)# network 192.168.1.0
R1(config-router)# no auto-summary
```

i. Configure EIGRP and a static default route on R2.

```
R2(config)# router eigrp 1
R2(config-router)# network 192.168.0.252 0.0.0.3
R2(config-router)# redistribute static
R2(config-router)# exit
R2(config)# ip route 0.0.0.0 0.0.0.0 209.165.200.225
```

j. Configure a summary static route on ISP to the networks on R1 and R2 routers.

```
ISP(config)# ip route 192.168.0.0 255.255.254.0 209.165.200.226
```

Step 4: Verify network connectivity between the routers.

If any pings between the routers fail, correct the errors before proceeding to the next step. Use **show ip route** and **show ip interface brief** to locate possible issues.

Step 5: Configure basic settings for each switch.

a. Disable DNS lookup.

b. Configure device name as shown in the topology.

c. Configure the IP address for the VLAN 1 interface and the default gateway for each switch.

d. Assign **class** as the privileged EXEC mode password.

e. Assign **cisco** as the console and vty passwords.

f. Configure **logging synchronous** for the console line.

Step 6: Verify the hosts are configured for DHCP.

Step 7: Load the initial DHCP configuration for R1 and R2.

Router R1

```
interface GigabitEthernet0/1
 ip helper-address 192.168.0.253
```

Router R2

```
ip dhcp excluded-address 192.168.11.1 192.168.11.9

ip dhcp excluded-address 192.168.0.1 192.168.0.9
ip dhcp pool R1G1
```

```
   network 192.168.1.0 255.255.255.0
   default-router 192.168.1.1
 ip dhcp pool R1G0
   network 192.168.0.0 255.255.255.128
   default-router 192.168.11.1
```

Part 2: Troubleshoot DHCPv4 Issues

After configuring routers R1 and R2 with DHCPv4 settings, several errors in the DHCP configurations were introduced and resulted in connectivity issues. R2 is configured as a DHCP server. For both pools of DHCP addresses, the first nine addresses are reserved for the routers and switches. R1 relays the DHCP information to all the R1 LANs. Currently, PC-A and PC-B have no access to the network. Use the **show** and **debug** commands to determine and correct the network connectivity issues.

Step 1:   Record IP settings for PC-A and PC-B.

a. For PC-A and PC-B, at the command prompt, enter **ipconfig /all** to display the IP and MAC addresses.

b. Record the IP and MAC addresses in the table below. The MAC address can be used to determine which PC is involved in the debug message.

	IP Address/Subnet Mask	MAC Address
PC-A		
PC-B		

Step 2:   Troubleshoot DHCP issues for the 192.168.1.0/24 network on router R1.

Router R1 is a DHCP relay agent for all the R1 LANs. In this step, only the DHCP process for the 192.168.1.0/24 network will be examined. The first nine addresses are reserved for other network devices, such as routers, switches, and servers.

a. Use a DHCP **debug** command to observe the DHCP process on R2 router.

```
R2# debug ip dhcp server events
```

b. On R1, display the running configuration for the G0/1 interface.

```
R1# show run interface g0/1
interface GigabitEthernet0/1
  ip address 192.168.1.1 255.255.255.0
  ip helper-address 192.168.0.253
  duplex auto
  speed auto
```

If there are any DHCP relay issues, record any commands that are necessary to correct the configurations errors.

_____

_____

_____

c. In a command prompt on PC-A, type **ipconfig /renew** to receive an address from the DHCP server. Record the configured IP address, subnet mask, and default gateway for PC-A.

_____

d. Observe the debug messages on R2 router for the DHCP renewal process for PC-A. The DHCP server attempted to assign 192.168.1.1/24 to PC-A. This address is already in use for G0/1 interface on R1. The same issue occurs with IP address 192.168.1.2/24 because this address has been assigned to S1 in the initial configuration. Therefore, an IP address of 192.168.1.3/24 has been assigned to PC-A. The DHCP assignment conflict indicates there may be an issue with the excluded-address statement on the DHCP server configuration on R2.

```
*Mar  5 06:32:16.939: DHCPD: Sending notification of DISCOVER:
*Mar  5 06:32:16.939:   DHCPD: htype 1 chaddr 0050.56be.768c
*Mar  5 06:32:16.939:   DHCPD: circuit id 00000000
*Mar  5 06:32:16.939: DHCPD: Seeing if there is an internally specified pool class:
*Mar  5 06:32:16.939:   DHCPD: htype 1 chaddr 0050.56be.768c
*Mar  5 06:32:16.939:   DHCPD: circuit id 00000000
*Mar  5 06:32:16.943: DHCPD: Allocated binding 2944C764
*Mar  5 06:32:16.943: DHCPD: Adding binding to radix tree (192.168.1.1)
*Mar  5 06:32:16.943: DHCPD: Adding binding to hash tree
*Mar  5 06:32:16.943: DHCPD: assigned IP address 192.168.1.1 to client 0100.5056.
be76.8c.
*Mar  5 06:32:16.951: %DHCPD-4-PING_CONFLICT: DHCP address conflict:  server pinged
192.168.1.1.
*Mar  5 06:32:16.951: DHCPD: returned 192.168.1.1 to address pool R1G1.
*Mar  5 06:32:16.951: DHCPD: Sending notification of DISCOVER:
*Mar  5 06:32:16.951:   DHCPD: htype 1 chaddr 0050.56be.768c
*Mar  5 06:32:16.951:   DHCPD: circuit id 00000000
*Mar  5 06:32:1
R2#6.951: DHCPD: Seeing if there is an internally specified pool class:
*Mar  5 06:32:16.951:   DHCPD: htype 1 chaddr 0050.56be.768c
*Mar  5 06:32:16.951:   DHCPD: circuit id 00000000
*Mar  5 06:32:16.951: DHCPD: Allocated binding 31DC93C8
*Mar  5 06:32:16.951: DHCPD: Adding binding to radix tree (192.168.1.2)
*Mar  5 06:32:16.951: DHCPD: Adding binding to hash tree
*Mar  5 06:32:16.951: DHCPD: assigned IP address 192.168.1.2 to client 0100.5056.
be76.8c.
*Mar  5 06:32:18.383: %DHCPD-4-PING_CONFLICT: DHCP address conflict:  server pinged
192.168.1.2.
*Mar  5 06:32:18.383: DHCPD: returned 192.168.1.2 to address pool R1G1.
*Mar  5 06:32:18.383: DHCPD: Sending notification of DISCOVER:
*Mar  5 06:32:18.383:   DHCPD: htype 1 chaddr 0050.56be.6c89
*Mar  5 06:32:18.383:   DHCPD: circuit id 00000000
*Mar  5 06:32:18.383: DHCPD: Seeing if there is an internally specified pool class:
```

```
*Mar  5 06:32:18.383:   DHCPD: htype 1 chaddr 0050.56be.6c89
*Mar  5 06:32:18.383:   DHCPD: circuit id 00000000
*Mar  5 06:32:18.383: DHCPD: Allocated binding 2A40E074
*Mar  5 06:32:18.383: DHCPD: Adding binding to radix tree (192.168.1.3)
*Mar  5 06:32:18.383: DHCPD: Adding binding to hash tree
*Mar  5 06:32:18.383: DHCPD: assigned IP address 192.168.1.3 to client 0100.5056.
be76.8c.
<output omitted>
```

e. Display the DHCP server configuration on R2. The first nine addresses for 192.168.1.0/24 network are not excluded from the DHCP pool.

R2# **show run | section dhcp**

```
ip dhcp excluded-address 192.168.11.1 192.168.11.9
ip dhcp excluded-address 192.168.0.1 192.168.0.9
ip dhcp pool R1G1
 network 192.168.1.0 255.255.255.0
 default-router 192.168.1.1
ip dhcp pool R1G0
 network 192.168.0.0 255.255.255.128
 default-router 192.168.1.1
```

Record the commands to resolve the issue on R2.

_____

_____

f. At the command prompt on PC-A, type **ipconfig /release** to return the 192.168.1.3 address back to the DHCP pool. The process can be observed in the debug message on R2.

```
*Mar  5 06:49:59.563:   DHCPD: Sending notification of TERMINATION:
*Mar  5 06:49:59.563:   DHCPD: address 192.168.1.3 mask 255.255.255.0
*Mar  5 06:49:59.563:   DHCPD: reason flags: RELEASE
*Mar  5 06:49:59.563:   DHCPD: htype 1 chaddr 0050.56be.768c
*Mar  5 06:49:59.563:   DHCPD: lease time remaining (secs) = 85340
*Mar  5 06:49:59.563:   DHCPD: returned 192.168.1.3 to address pool R1G1.
```

g. At the command prompt on PC-A, type **ipconfig /renew** to be assigned a new IP address from the DHCP server. Record the assigned IP address and default gateway information.

_____

The process can be observed in the debug message on R2.

```
*Mar  5 06:50:11.863:   DHCPD: Sending notification of DISCOVER:
*Mar  5 06:50:11.863:   DHCPD: htype 1 chaddr 0050.56be.768c
*Mar  5 06:50:11.863:   DHCPD: circuit id 00000000
*Mar  5 06:50:11.863:   DHCPD: Seeing if there is an internally specified pool class:
*Mar  5 06:50:11.863:   DHCPD: htype 1 chaddr 0050.56be.768c
*Mar  5 06:50:11.863:   DHCPD: circuit id 00000000
*Mar  5 06:50:11.863:   DHCPD: requested address 192.168.1.3 has already been assigned.
*Mar  5 06:50:11.863:   DHCPD: Allocated binding 3003018C
*Mar  5 06:50:11.863:   DHCPD: Adding binding to radix tree (192.168.1.10)
*Mar  5 06:50:11.863:   DHCPD: Adding binding to hash tree
*Mar  5 06:50:11.863:   DHCPD: assigned IP address 192.168.1.10 to client 0100.5056.
be76.8c.
<output omitted>
```

h. Verify network connectivity.

Can PC-A ping the assigned default gateway? _____

Can PC-A ping the R2 router? _____

Can PC-A ping the ISP router? _____

Step 3: Troubleshoot DHCP issues for 192.168.0.0/25 network on R1.

Router R1 is a DHCP relay agent for all the R1 LANs. In this step, only the DHCP process for the 192.168.0.0/25 network is examined. The first nine addresses are reserved for other network devices.

a. Use a DHCP **debug** command to observe the DHCP process on R2.

```
R2# debug ip dhcp server events
```

b. Display the running configuration for the G0/0 interface on R1 to identify possible DHCP issues.

```
R1# show run interface g0/0
interface GigabitEthernet0/0
 ip address 192.168.0.1 255.255.255.128
 duplex auto
 speed auto
```

Record the issues and any commands that are necessary to correct the configurations errors.

_____

_____

_____

c. From the command prompt on PC-B, type **ipconfig /renew** to receive an address from the DHCP server. Record the configured IP address, subnet mask, and default gateway for PC-B.

_____

d. Observe the debug messages on R2 router for the renewal process for PC-A. The DHCP server assigned 192.168.0.10/25 to PC-B.

```
*Mar  5 07:15:09.663:  DHCPD: Sending notification of DISCOVER:
*Mar  5 07:15:09.663:  DHCPD: htype 1 chaddr 0050.56be.f6db
*Mar  5 07:15:09.663:  DHCPD: circuit id 00000000
*Mar  5 07:15:09.663:  DHCPD: Seeing if there is an internally specified pool class:
*Mar  5 07:15:09.663:  DHCPD: htype 1 chaddr 0050.56be.f6db
*Mar  5 07:15:09.663:  DHCPD: circuit id 00000000
*Mar  5 07:15:09.707:  DHCPD: Sending notification of ASSIGNMENT:
*Mar  5 07:15:09.707:  DHCPD: address 192.168.0.10 mask 255.255.255.128
*Mar  5 07:15:09.707:  DHCPD: htype 1 chaddr 0050.56be.f6db
*Mar  5 07:15:09.707:  DHCPD: lease time remaining (secs) = 86400
```

e. Verify network connectivity.

Can PC-B ping the DHCP assigned default gateway? _____

Can PC-B ping its default gateway (192.168.0.1)? _____

Can PC-B ping the R2 router? _____

Can PC-B ping the ISP router? _____

f. If any issues failed in Step e, record the problems and any commands to resolve the issues.

_____

_____

g. Release and renew the IP configurations on PC-B. Repeat Step e to verify network connectivity.

h. Discontinue the debug process by using the **undebug all** command.

```
R2# undebug all
All possible debugging has been turned off
```

Reflection

What are the benefits of using DHCP?

_____

_____

Router Interface Summary Table

Router Interface Summary				
Router Model	**Ethernet Interface #1**	**Ethernet Interface #2**	**Serial Interface #1**	**Serial Interface #2**
1800	Fast Ethernet 0/0 (F0/0)	Fast Ethernet 0/1 (F0/1)	Serial 0/0/0 (S0/0/0)	Serial 0/0/1 (S0/0/1)
1900	Gigabit Ethernet 0/0 (G0/0)	Gigabit Ethernet 0/1 (G0/1)	Serial 0/0/0 (S0/0/0)	Serial 0/0/1 (S0/0/1)
2801	Fast Ethernet 0/0 (F0/0)	Fast Ethernet 0/1 (F0/1)	Serial 0/1/0 (S0/1/0)	Serial 0/1/1 (S0/1/1)
2811	Fast Ethernet 0/0 (F0/0)	Fast Ethernet 0/1 (F0/1)	Serial 0/0/0 (S0/0/0)	Serial 0/0/1 (S0/0/1)
2900	Gigabit Ethernet 0/0 (G0/0)	Gigabit Ethernet 0/1 (G0/1)	Serial 0/0/0 (S0/0/0)	Serial 0/0/1 (S0/0/1)
Note: To find out how the router is configured, look at the interfaces to identify the type of router and how many interfaces the router has. There is no way to effectively list all the combinations of configurations for each router class. This table includes identifiers for the possible combinations of Ethernet and Serial interfaces in the device. The table does not include any other type of interface, even though a specific router may contain one. An example of this might be an ISDN BRI interface. The string in parenthesis is the legal abbreviation that can be used in Cisco IOS commands to represent the interface.				

7.2.3.5 Lab – Configuring Stateless and Stateful DHCPv6

Topology

Addressing Table

Device	Interface	IPv6 Address	Prefix Length	Default Gateway
R1	G0/1	2001:DB8:ACAD:A::1	64	N/A
S1	VLAN 1	Assigned by SLAAC	64	Assigned by SLAAC
PC-A	NIC	Assigned by SLAAC and DHCPv6	64	Assigned by R1

Objectives

Part 1: Build the Network and Configure Basic Device Settings

Part 2: Configure the Network for SLAAC

Part 3: Configure the Network for Stateless DHCPv6

Part 4: Configure the Network for Stateful DHCPv6

Background / Scenario

The dynamic assignment of IPv6 global unicast addresses can be configured in three ways:

- Stateless Address Autoconfiguration (SLAAC) only
- Stateless Dynamic Host Configuration Protocol for IPv6 (DHCPv6)
- Stateful DHCPv6

With SLAAC (pronounced slack), a DHCPv6 server is not needed for hosts to acquire IPv6 addresses. It can be used to receive additional information that the host needs, such as the domain name and the domain name server (DNS) address. When SLAAC is used to assign the IPv6 host addresses and DHCPv6 is used to assign other network parameters, it is called Stateless DHCPv6.

With Stateful DHCPv6, the DHCP server assigns all information, including the host IPv6 address.

Determination of how hosts obtain their dynamic IPv6 addressing information is dependent on flag settings contained within the router advertisement (RA) messages.

In this lab, you will initially configure the network to use SLAAC. After connectivity has been verified, you will configure DHCPv6 settings and change the network to use Stateless DHCPv6. After verification that Stateless DHCPv6 is functioning correctly, you will change the configuration on R1 to use Stateful DHCPv6. Wireshark will be used on PC-A to verify all three dynamic network configurations.

Note: The routers used with CCNA hands-on labs are Cisco 1941 Integrated Services Routers (ISRs) with Cisco IOS Release 15.2(4)M3 (universalk9 image). The switches used are Cisco Catalyst 2960s with Cisco IOS Release 15.0(2) (lanbasek9 image). Other routers, switches and Cisco IOS versions can be used. Depending on the model and Cisco IOS version, the commands available and output produced might vary from what is shown in the labs. Refer to the Router Interface Summary Table at the end of this lab for the correct interface identifiers.

Note: Make sure that the router and switch have been erased and have no startup configurations. If you are unsure, contact your instructor.

Note: The **default bias** template (used by the Switch Database Manager (SDM)) does not provide IPv6 address capabilities. Verify that SDM is using either the **dual-ipv4-and-ipv6** template or the **lanbase-routing** template. The new template will be used after reboot even if the config is not saved.

> S1# **show sdm prefer**

Follow these steps to assign the **dual-ipv4-and-ipv6** template as the default SDM template:

> S1# **config t**
> S1(config)# **sdm prefer dual-ipv4-and-ipv6 default**
> S1(config)# **end**
> S1# **reload**

Required Resources

- 1 Router (Cisco 1941 with Cisco IOS Release 15.2(4)M3 universal image or comparable)
- 1 Switch (Cisco 2960 with Cisco IOS Release 15.0(2) lanbasek9 image or comparable)
- 1 PC (Windows 7 or Vista with Wireshark and terminal emulation program, such as Tera Term)
- Console cables to configure the Cisco IOS devices via the console ports
- Ethernet cables as shown in the topology

Note: DHCPv6 client services are disabled on Windows XP. It is recommended to use a Windows 7 host for this lab.

Part 1:   Build the Network and Configure Basic Device Settings

In Part 1, you will set up the network topology and configure basic settings, such as device names, passwords and interface IP addresses.

Step 1:   Cable the network as shown in the topology.

Step 2:   Initialize and reload the router and switch as necessary.

Step 3:   Configure R1.

a.   Disable DNS lookup.

b.   Configure the device name.

c.   Encrypt plain text passwords.

d.   Create a MOTD banner warning users that unauthorized access is prohibited.

e. Assign **class** as the encrypted privileged EXEC mode password.

f. Assign **cisco** as the console and vty password and enable login.

g. Set console logging to synchronous mode.

h. Save the running configuration to the startup configuration.

Step 4: Configure S1.

a. Disable DNS lookup.

b. Configure the device name.

c. Encrypt plain text passwords.

d. Create a MOTD banner warning users that unauthorized access is prohibited.

e. Assign **class** as the encrypted privileged EXEC mode password.

f. Assign **cisco** as the console and vty password and enable login.

g. Set console logging to synchronous mode.

h. Administratively disable all inactive interfaces.

i. Save running configuration to the startup configuration.

Part 2: Configure the Network for SLAAC

Step 1: Prepare PC-A.

a. Verify that the IPv6 protocol has been enabled on the Local Area Connection Properties window. If the Internet Protocol Version 6 (TCP/IPv6) check box is not checked, click to enable it.

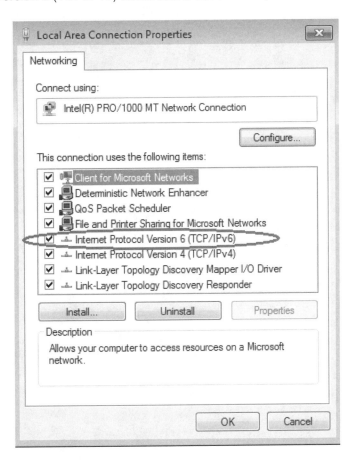

b. Start a Wireshark capture of traffic on the NIC.

c. Filter the data capture to see only RA messages. This can be done by filtering on IPv6 packets with a destination address of FF02::1, which is the all-unicast client group address. The filter entry used with Wireshark is **ipv6.dst==ff02::1**, as shown here.

Step 2: Configure R1.

a. Enable IPv6 unicast routing.

b. Assign the IPv6 unicast address to interface G0/1 according to the Addressing Table.

c. Assign FE80::1 as the IPv6 link-local address for interface G0/1.

d. Activate interface G0/1.

Step 3: Verify that R1 is part of the all-router multicast group.

Use the **show ipv6 interface g0/1** command to verify that G0/1 is part of the All-router multicast group (FF02::2). RA messages are not sent out G0/1 without that group assignment.

```
R1# show ipv6 interface g0/1
GigabitEthernet0/1 is up, line protocol is up
  IPv6 is enabled, link-local address is FE80::1
  No Virtual link-local address(es):
  Global unicast address(es):
    2001:DB8:ACAD:A::1, subnet is 2001:DB8:ACAD:A::/64
  Joined group address(es):
    FF02::1
    FF02::2
    FF02::1:FF00:1
  MTU is 1500 bytes
  ICMP error messages limited to one every 100 milliseconds
  ICMP redirects are enabled
  ICMP unreachables are sent
  ND DAD is enabled, number of DAD attempts: 1
  ND reachable time is 30000 milliseconds (using 30000)
  ND advertised reachable time is 0 (unspecified)
  ND advertised retransmit interval is 0 (unspecified)
  ND router advertisements are sent every 200 seconds
  ND router advertisements live for 1800 seconds
  ND advertised default router preference is Medium
  Hosts use stateless autoconfig for addresses.
```

Step 4: Configure S1.

Use the **ipv6 address autoconfig** command on VLAN 1 to obtain an IPv6 address through SLAAC.

```
S1(config)# interface vlan 1
S1(config-if)# ipv6 address autoconfig
S1(config-if)# end
```

Step 5:   Verify that SLAAC provided a unicast address to S1.

Use the **show ipv6 interface** command to verify that SLAAC provided a unicast address to VLAN1 on S1.

```
S1# show ipv6 interface
Vlan1 is up, line protocol is up
  IPv6 is enabled, link-local address is FE80::ED9:96FF:FEE8:8A40
  No Virtual link-local address(es):
  Stateless address autoconfig enabled
  Global unicast address(es):
    2001:DB8:ACAD:A:ED9:96FF:FEE8:8A40, subnet is 2001:DB8:ACAD:A::/64 [EUI/CAL/PRE]
      valid lifetime 2591988 preferred lifetime 604788
  Joined group address(es):
    FF02::1
    FF02::1:FFE8:8A40
  MTU is 1500 bytes
  ICMP error messages limited to one every 100 milliseconds
  ICMP redirects are enabled
  ICMP unreachables are sent
  Output features: Check hwidb
  ND DAD is enabled, number of DAD attempts: 1
  ND reachable time is 30000 milliseconds (using 30000)
  ND NS retransmit interval is 1000 milliseconds
  Default router is FE80::1 on Vlan1
```

Step 6:   Verify that SLAAC provided IPv6 address information on PC-A.

a.   From a command prompt on PC-A, issue the **ipconfig /all** command. Verify that PC-A is showing an IPv6 address with the 2001:db8:acad:a::/64 prefix. The Default Gateway should have the FE80::1 address.

b.   From Wireshark, look at one of the RA messages that were captured. Expand the Internet Control Message Protocol v6 layer to view the Flags and Prefix information. The first two flags control DHCPv6 usage and are not set if DHCPv6 is not configured. The prefix information is also contained within this RA message.

```
Filter:  ipv6.dst==ff02::1                                    ▼  Expression... Clear Apply

No.     Time       Source          Destination        Protocol Length Info
 3518 3972.07973 fe80::1           ff02::1            ICMPv6    118 Router Advertisement from d4:8c:b5:ce:a0:c1
 3673 4130.43155 fe80::1           ff02::1            ICMPv6    118 Router Advertisement from d4:8c:b5:ce:a0:c1
 3840 4284.68370 fe80::1           ff02::1            ICMPv6    118 Router Advertisement from d4:8c:b5:ce:a0:c1
 3989 4435.87602 fe80::1           ff02::1            ICMPv6    118 Router Advertisement from d4:8c:b5:ce:a0:c1
⊞ Frame 3518: 118 bytes on wire (944 bits), 118 bytes captured (944 bits)
⊞ Ethernet II, Src: d4:8c:b5:ce:a0:c1 (d4:8c:b5:ce:a0:c1), Dst: IPv6mcast_00:00:00:01 (33:33:00:00:00:01)
⊞ Internet Protocol Version 6, Src: fe80::1 (fe80::1), Dst: ff02::1 (ff02::1)
⊟ Internet Control Message Protocol v6
    Type: Router Advertisement (134)
    Code: 0
    Checksum: 0x1816 [correct]
    Cur hop limit: 64
  ⊟ Flags: 0x00
      0... .... = Managed address configuration: Not set
      .0.. .... = Other configuration: Not set
      ..0. .... = Home Agent: Not set
      ...0 0... = Prf (Default Router Preference): Medium (0)
      .... .0.. = Proxy: Not set
      .... ..0. = Reserved: 0
    Router lifetime (s): 1800
    Reachable time (ms): 0
    Retrans timer (ms): 0
  ⊞ ICMPv6 Option (Source link-layer address : d4:8c:b5:ce:a0:c1)
  ⊞ ICMPv6 Option (MTU : 1500)
  ⊟ ICMPv6 Option (Prefix information : 2001:db8:acad:a::/64)
      Type: Prefix information (3)
      Length: 4 (32 bytes)
      Prefix Length: 64
    ⊞ Flag: 0xc0
      Valid Lifetime: 2592000
      Preferred Lifetime: 604800
      Reserved
      Prefix: 2001:db8:acad:a:: (2001:db8:acad:a::)
```

Part 3:   Configure the Network for Stateless DHCPv6

Step 1:   Configure an IPv6 DHCP server on R1.

a. Create an IPv6 DHCP pool.

```
R1(config)# ipv6 dhcp pool IPV6POOL-A
```

b. Assign a domain name to the pool.

```
R1(config-dhcpv6)# domain-name ccna-statelessDHCPv6.com
```

c. Assign a DNS server address.

```
R1(config-dhcpv6)# dns-server 2001:db8:acad:a::abcd
R1(config-dhcpv6)# exit
```

d. Assign the DHCPv6 pool to the interface.

```
R1(config)# interface g0/1
R1(config-if)# ipv6 dhcp server IPV6POOL-A
```

e. Set the DHCPv6 network discovery (ND) **other-config-flag**.

```
R1(config-if)# ipv6 nd other-config-flag
R1(config-if)# end
```

Step 2:   Verify DHCPv6 settings on interface G0/1 on R1.

Use the **show ipv6 interface g0/1** command to verify that the interface is now part of the IPv6 multicast all-DHCPv6-servers group (FF02::1:2). The last line of the output from this **show** command verifies that the other-config-flag has been set.

```
R1# show ipv6 interface g0/1
GigabitEthernet0/1 is up, line protocol is up
  IPv6 is enabled, link-local address is FE80::1
  No Virtual link-local address(es):
  Global unicast address(es):
```

```
     2001:DB8:ACAD:A::1, subnet is 2001:DB8:ACAD:A::/64
Joined group address(es):
  FF02::1
  FF02::2
  FF02::1:2
  FF02::1:FF00:1
  FF05::1:3
MTU is 1500 bytes
ICMP error messages limited to one every 100 milliseconds
ICMP redirects are enabled
ICMP unreachables are sent
ND DAD is enabled, number of DAD attempts: 1
ND reachable time is 30000 milliseconds (using 30000)
ND advertised reachable time is 0 (unspecified)
ND advertised retransmit interval is 0 (unspecified)
ND router advertisements are sent every 200 seconds
ND router advertisements live for 1800 seconds
ND advertised default router preference is Medium
Hosts use stateless autoconfig for addresses.
Hosts use DHCP to obtain other configuration.
```

Step 3: View network changes to PC-A.

Use the **ipconfig /all** command to review the network changes. Notice that additional information, including the domain name and DNS server information, has been retrieved from the DHCPv6 server. However, the IPv6 global unicast and link-local addresses were obtained previously from SLAAC.

```
Ethernet adapter Local Area Connection:

   Connection-specific DNS Suffix  . : ccna-statelessDHCPv6.com
   Description . . . . . . . . . . . : Intel(R) PRO/1000 MT Network Connection
   Physical Address. . . . . . . . . : 00-50-56-BE-76-8C
   DHCP Enabled. . . . . . . . . . . : Yes
   Autoconfiguration Enabled . . . . : Yes
   IPv6 Address. . . . . . . . . . . : 2001:db8:acad:a:24ba:a0a0:9f0:ff88(Prefer
red)
   Temporary IPv6 Address. . . . . . : 2001:db8:acad:a:103a:4344:4b5e:ab1d(Prefe
rred)
   Link-local IPv6 Address . . . . . : fe80::24ba:a0a0:9f0:ff88%11(Preferred)
   Autoconfiguration IPv4 Address. . : 169.254.255.136(Preferred)
   Subnet Mask . . . . . . . . . . . : 255.255.0.0
   Default Gateway . . . . . . . . . : fe80::1%11
   DHCPv6 IAID . . . . . . . . . . . : 234884137
   DHCPv6 Client DUID. . . . . . . . : 00-01-00-01-17-F6-72-3D-00-0C-29-8D-54-44

   DNS Servers . . . . . . . . . . . : 2001:db8:acad:a::abcd
   NetBIOS over Tcpip. . . . . . . . : Enabled
   Connection-specific DNS Suffix Search List :
                                       ccna-statelessDHCPv6.com

Tunnel adapter isatap.{E2FC1866-B195-460A-BF40-F04F42A38FFE}:

   Media State . . . . . . . . . . . : Media disconnected
   Connection-specific DNS Suffix  . : ccna-statelessDHCPv6.com
   Description . . . . . . . . . . . : Microsoft ISATAP Adapter
   Physical Address. . . . . . . . . : 00-00-00-00-00-00-00-E0
   DHCP Enabled. . . . . . . . . . . : No
   Autoconfiguration Enabled . . . . : Yes
```

Step 4: View the RA messages in Wireshark.

Scroll down to the last RA message that is displayed in Wireshark and expand it to view the ICMPv6 flag settings. Notice that the other configuration flag is set to 1.

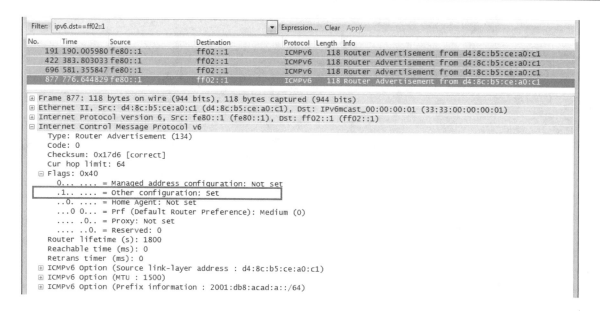

Step 5: Verify that PC-A did not obtain its IPv6 address from a DHCPv6 server.

Use the **show ipv6 dhcp binding** and **show ipv6 dhcp pool** commands to verify that PC-A did not obtain an IPv6 address from the DHCPv6 pool.

```
R1# show ipv6 dhcp binding
R1# show ipv6 dhcp pool
DHCPv6 pool: IPV6POOL-A
   DNS server: 2001:DB8:ACAD:A::ABCD
   Domain name: ccna-statelessDHCPv6.com
   Active clients: 0
```

Step 6: Reset PC-A IPv6 network settings.

a. Shut down interface F0/6 on S1.

Note: Shutting down the interface F0/6 prevents PC-A from receiving a new IPv6 address before you reconfigure R1 for Stateful DHCPv6 in Part 4.

```
S1(config)# interface f0/6
S1(config-if)# shutdown
```

b. Stop Wireshark capture of traffic on the PC-A NIC.

c. Reset the IPv6 settings on PC-A to remove the Stateless DHCPv6 settings.

1) Open the Local Area Connection Properties window, deselect the **Internet Protocol Version 6 (TCP/IPv6)** check box, and click **OK** to accept the change.

2) Open the Local Area Connection Properties window again, click to enable the **Internet Protocol Version 6 (TCP/IPv6)** check box, and then click **OK** to accept the change.

Part 4: Configure the Network for Stateful DHCPv6

Step 1: Prepare PC-A.

a. Start a Wireshark capture of traffic on the NIC.

b. Filter the data capture to see only RA messages. This can be done by filtering on IPv6 packets with a destination address of FF02::1, which is the all-unicast client group address.

Filter: ipv6.dst==ff02::1   ▼ Expression... Clear Apply

Step 2: Change the DHCPv6 pool on R1.

a. Add the network prefix to the pool.

```
R1(config)# ipv6 dhcp pool IPV6POOL-A
R1(config-dhcpv6)# address prefix 2001:db8:acad:a::/64
```

b. Change the domain name to **ccna-statefulDHCPv6.com**.

Note: You must remove the old domain name. It is not replaced by the **domain-name** command.

```
R1(config-dhcpv6)# no domain-name ccna-statelessDHCPv6.com
R1(config-dhcpv6)# domain-name ccna-StatefulDHCPv6.com
R1(config-dhcpv6)# end
```

c. Verify DHCPv6 pool settings.

```
R1# show ipv6 dhcp pool
DHCPv6 pool: IPV6POOL-A
  Address allocation prefix: 2001:DB8:ACAD:A::/64 valid 172800 preferred 86400 (0 in
use, 0 conflicts)
  DNS server: 2001:DB8:ACAD:A::ABCD
  Domain name: ccna-StatefulDHCPv6.com
  Active clients: 0
```

d. Enter debug mode to verify the Stateful DHCPv6 address assignment.

```
R1# debug ipv6 dhcp detail
    IPv6 DHCP debugging is on (detailed)
```

Step 3: Set the flag on G0/1 for Stateful DHCPv6.

Note: Shutting down the G0/1 interface before making changes ensures that an RA message is sent when the interface is activated.

```
R1(config)# interface g0/1
R1(config-if)# shutdown
R1(config-if)# ipv6 nd managed-config-flag
R1(config-if)# no shutdown
R1(config-if)# end
```

Step 4: Enable interface F0/6 on S1.

Now that R1 has been configured for Stateful DHCPv6, you can reconnect PC-A to the network by activating interface F0/6 on S1.

```
S1(config)# interface f0/6
S1(config-if)# no shutdown
S1(config-if)# end
```

Step 5: Verify Stateful DHCPv6 settings on R1.

a. Issue the **show ipv6 interface g0/1** command to verify that the interface is in Stateful DHCPv6 mode.

```
R1# show ipv6 interface g0/1
GigabitEthernet0/1 is up, line protocol is up
   IPv6 is enabled, link-local address is FE80::1
```

```
No Virtual link-local address(es):
Global unicast address(es):
   2001:DB8:ACAD:A::1, subnet is 2001:DB8:ACAD:A::/64
Joined group address(es):
   FF02::1
   FF02::2
   FF02::1:2
   FF02::1:FF00:1
   FF05::1:3
MTU is 1500 bytes
ICMP error messages limited to one every 100 milliseconds
ICMP redirects are enabled
ICMP unreachables are sent
ND DAD is enabled, number of DAD attempts: 1
ND reachable time is 30000 milliseconds (using 30000)
ND advertised reachable time is 0 (unspecified)
ND advertised retransmit interval is 0 (unspecified)
ND router advertisements are sent every 200 seconds
ND router advertisements live for 1800 seconds
ND advertised default router preference is Medium
Hosts use DHCP to obtain routable addresses.
Hosts use DHCP to obtain other configuration.
```

b. In a command prompt on PC-A, type **ipconfig /release6** to release the currently assigned IPv6 address. Then type **ipconfig /renew6** to request an IPv6 address from the DHCPv6 server.

c. Issue the **show ipv6 dhcp pool** command to verify the number of active clients.

```
R1# show ipv6 dhcp pool
DHCPv6 pool: IPV6POOL-A
   Address allocation prefix: 2001:DB8:ACAD:A::/64 valid 172800 preferred 86400 (1 in
use, 0 conflicts)
   DNS server: 2001:DB8:ACAD:A::ABCD
   Domain name: ccna-StatefulDHCPv6.com
   Active clients: 1
```

d. Issue the **show ipv6 dhcp binding** command to verify that PC-A received its IPv6 unicast address from the DHCP pool. Compare the client address to the link-local IPv6 address on PC-A using the **ipconfig / all** command. Compare the address provided by the **show** command to the IPv6 address listed with the **ipconfig /all** command on PC-A.

```
R1# show ipv6 dhcp binding
Client: FE80::D428:7DE2:997C:B05A
   DUID: 0001000117F6723D000C298D5444
   Username : unassigned
   IA NA: IA ID 0x0E000C29, T1 43200, T2 69120
      Address: 2001:DB8:ACAD:A:B55C:8519:8915:57CE
               preferred lifetime 86400, valid lifetime 172800
               expires at Mar 07 2013 04:09 PM (171595 seconds)
```

```
Ethernet adapter Local Area Connection:

    Connection-specific DNS Suffix  . : ccna-StatefulDHCPv6.com
    Description . . . . . . . . . . . : Intel(R) PRO/1000 MT Network Connection
    Physical Address. . . . . . . . . : 00-50-56-BE-6C-89
    DHCP Enabled. . . . . . . . . . . : Yes
    Autoconfiguration Enabled . . . . : Yes
    IPv6 Address. . . . . . . . . . . : 2001:db8:acad:a:b55c:8519:8915:57ce(Prefe
rred)
    Lease Obtained. . . . . . . . . . : Tuesday, March 05, 2013 11:53:11 AM
    Lease Expires . . . . . . . . . . : Thursday, March 07, 2013 11:53:11 AM
    IPv6 Address. . . . . . . . . . . : 2001:db8:acad:a:d428:7de2:997c:b05a(Prefe
rred)
    Temporary IPv6 Address. . . . . . : 2001:db8:acad:a:dd37:1e42:948c:225b(Prefe
rred)
    Link-local IPv6 Address . . . . . : fe80::d428:7de2:997c:b05a%11(Preferred)
    Autoconfiguration IPv4 Address. . : 169.254.176.90(Preferred)
    Subnet Mask . . . . . . . . . . . : 255.255.0.0
    Default Gateway . . . . . . . . . : fe80::1%11
    DHCPv6 IAID . . . . . . . . . . . : 234884137
    DHCPv6 Client DUID. . . . . . . . : 00-01-00-01-17-F6-72-3D-00-0C-29-8D-54-44

    DNS Servers . . . . . . . . . . . : 2001:db8:acad:a::abcd
    NetBIOS over Tcpip. . . . . . . . : Enabled
    Connection-specific DNS Suffix Search List :
                                        ccna-StatefulDHCPv6.com
```

e. Issue the **undebug all** command on R1 to stop debugging DHCPv6.

Note: Typing **u all** is the shortest form of this command and is useful to know if you are trying to stop debug messages from continually scrolling down your terminal session screen. If multiple debugs are in process, the **undebug all** command stops all of them.

```
R1# u all
All possible debugging has been turned off
```

f. Review the debug messages that appeared on your R1 terminal screen.

1) Examine the solicit message from PC-A requesting network information.

```
*Mar  5 16:42:39.775: IPv6 DHCP: Received SOLICIT from FE80::D428:7DE2:997C:B05A on
GigabitEthernet0/1
*Mar  5 16:42:39.775: IPv6 DHCP: detailed packet contents
*Mar  5 16:42:39.775:   src FE80::D428:7DE2:997C:B05A (GigabitEthernet0/1)
*Mar  5 16:42:39.775:   dst FF02::1:2
*Mar  5 16:42:39.775:   type SOLICIT(1), xid 1039238
*Mar  5 16:42:39.775:   option ELAPSED-TIME(8), len 2
*Mar  5 16:42:39.775:     elapsed-time 6300
*Mar  5 16:42:39.775:   option CLIENTID(1), len 14
```

2) Examine the reply message sent back to PC-A with the DHCP network information.

```
*Mar  5 16:42:39.779: IPv6 DHCP: Sending REPLY to FE80::D428:7DE2:997C:B05A on
GigabitEthernet0/1
*Mar  5 16:42:39.779: IPv6 DHCP: detailed packet contents
*Mar  5 16:42:39.779:   src FE80::1
*Mar  5 16:42:39.779:   dst FE80::D428:7DE2:997C:B05A (GigabitEthernet0/1)
*Mar  5 16:42:39.779:   type REPLY(7), xid 1039238
*Mar  5 16:42:39.779:   option SERVERID(2), len 10
*Mar  5 16:42:39.779:     00030001FC994775C3E0
*Mar  5 16:42:39.779:   option CLIENTID(1), len 14
*Mar  5 16:42:39.779:     00010001
R1#17F6723D000C298D5444
*Mar  5 16:42:39.779:   option IA-NA(3), len 40
*Mar  5 16:42:39.779:     IAID 0x0E000C29, T1 43200, T2 69120
*Mar  5 16:42:39.779:     option IAADDR(5), len 24
*Mar  5 16:42:39.779:       IPv6 address 2001:DB8:ACAD:A:B55C:8519:8915:57CE
```

```
*Mar  5 16:42:39.779:        preferred 86400, valid 172800
*Mar  5 16:42:39.779:    option DNS-SERVERS(23), len 16
*Mar  5 16:42:39.779:       2001:DB8:ACAD:A::ABCD
*Mar  5 16:42:39.779:    option DOMAIN-LIST(24), len 26
*Mar  5 16:42:39.779:       ccna-StatefulDHCPv6.com
```

Step 6:   Verify Stateful DHCPv6 on PC-A

a.   Stop the Wireshark capture on PC-A.

b.   Expand the most recent RA message listed in Wireshark. Verify that the **Managed address configuration** flag has been set.

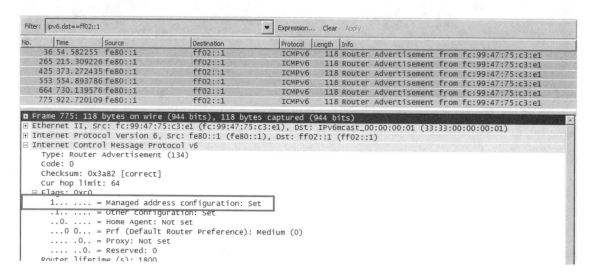

c.   Change the filter in Wireshark to view **DHCPv6** packets only by typing **dhcpv6**, and then **Apply** the filter. Highlight the last DHCPv6 reply listed and expand the DHCPv6 information. Examine the DHCPv6 network information that is contained in this packet.

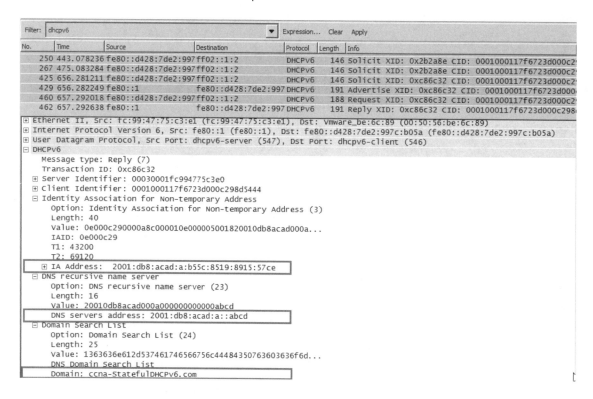

Reflection

1. What IPv6 addressing method uses more memory resources on the router configured as a DHCPv6 server, Stateless DHCPv6 or Stateful DHCPv6? Why?

    _____

    _____

    _____

2. Which type of dynamic IPv6 address assignment is recommended by Cisco, Stateless DHCPv6 or Stateful DHCPv6?

    _____

    _____

Router Interface Summary Table

Router Interface Summary				
Router Model	**Ethernet Interface #1**	**Ethernet Interface #2**	**Serial Interface #1**	**Serial Interface #2**
1800	Fast Ethernet 0/0 (F0/0)	Fast Ethernet 0/1 (F0/1)	Serial 0/0/0 (S0/0/0)	Serial 0/0/1 (S0/0/1)
1900	Gigabit Ethernet 0/0 (G0/0)	Gigabit Ethernet 0/1 (G0/1)	Serial 0/0/0 (S0/0/0)	Serial 0/0/1 (S0/0/1)
2801	Fast Ethernet 0/0 (F0/0)	Fast Ethernet 0/1 (F0/1)	Serial 0/1/0 (S0/1/0)	Serial 0/1/1 (S0/1/1)
2811	Fast Ethernet 0/0 (F0/0)	Fast Ethernet 0/1 (F0/1)	Serial 0/0/0 (S0/0/0)	Serial 0/0/1 (S0/0/1)
2900	Gigabit Ethernet 0/0 (G0/0)	Gigabit Ethernet 0/1 (G0/1)	Serial 0/0/0 (S0/0/0)	Serial 0/0/1 (S0/0/1)

Note: To find out how the router is configured, look at the interfaces to identify the type of router and how many interfaces the router has. There is no way to effectively list all the combinations of configurations for each router class. This table includes identifiers for the possible combinations of Ethernet and Serial interfaces in the device. The table does not include any other type of interface, even though a specific router may contain one. An example of this might be an ISDN BRI interface. The string in parenthesis is the legal abbreviation that can be used in Cisco IOS commands to represent the interface.

7.2.4.4 Lab - Troubleshooting DHCPv6

Topology

Addressing Table

Device	Interface	IPv6 Address	Prefix Length	Default Gateway
R1	G0/1	2001:DB8:ACAD:A::1	64	N/A
S1	VLAN 1	Assigned by SLAAC	64	Assigned by SLAAC
PC-A	NIC	Assigned by SLAAC and DHCPv6	64	Assigned by SLAAC

Objectives

Part 1: Build the Network and Configure Basic Device Settings

Part 2: Troubleshoot IPv6 Connectivity

Part 3: Troubleshoot Stateless DHCPv6

Background / Scenario

The ability to troubleshoot network issues is a very useful skill for network administrators. It is important to understand IPv6 address groups and how they are used when troubleshooting a network. Knowing what commands to use to extract IPv6 network information is necessary to effectively troubleshoot.

In this lab, you will load configurations on R1 and S1. These configurations will contain issues that prevent Stateless DHCPv6 from functioning on the network. You will troubleshoot R1 and S1 to resolve these issues.

Note: The routers used with CCNA hands-on labs are Cisco 1941 Integrated Services Routers (ISRs) with Cisco IOS Release 15.2(4)M3 (universalk9 image). The switches used are Cisco Catalyst 2960s with Cisco IOS Release 15.0(2) (lanbasek9 image). Other routers, switches and Cisco IOS versions can be used. Depending on the model and Cisco IOS version, the commands available and output produced might vary from what is shown in the labs. Refer to the Router Interface Summary Table at the end of this lab for the correct interface identifiers.

Note: Make sure that the router and switch have been erased and have no startup configurations. If you are unsure, contact your instructor.

Note: The default bias template used by the Switch Database Manager (SDM) does not provide IPv6 address capabilities. Verify that SDM is using either the **dual-ipv4-and-ipv6** template or the **lanbase-routing** template. The new template will be used after reboot even if the configuration is not saved.

```
S1# show sdm prefer
```

Follow this configuration to assign the **dual-ipv4-and-ipv6** template as the default SDM template:

```
S1# config t
S1(config)# sdm prefer dual-ipv4-and-ipv6 default
S1(config)# end
S1# reload
```

Required Resources

- 1 Router (Cisco 1941 with Cisco IOS Release 15.2(4)M3 universal image or comparable)
- 1 Switch (Cisco 2960 with Cisco IOS Release 15.0(2) lanbasek9 image or comparable)
- 1 PC (Windows 7, Vista, or XP with terminal emulation program, such as Tera Term)
- Console cables to configure the Cisco IOS devices via the console ports
- Ethernet cables as shown in the topology

Part 1: Build the Network and Configure Basic Device Settings

In Part 1, you will set up the network topology and clear any configurations if necessary. You will configure basic settings on the router and switch. Then you will load the provided IPv6 configurations before you start troubleshooting.

Step 1: Cable the network as shown in the topology.

Step 2: Initialize and reload the router and the switch.

Step 3: Configure basic settings on the router and switch.

a. Disable DNS lookup.

b. Configure device names as shown in the topology.

c. Encrypt plain text passwords.

d. Create a MOTD banner warning users that unauthorized access is prohibited.

e. Assign **class** as the encrypted privileged EXEC mode password.

f. Assign **cisco** as the console and vty passwords and enable login.

g. Configure **logging synchronous** to prevent console messages from interrupting command entry.

Step 4: Load the IPv6 configuration to R1.

```
ip domain name ccna-lab.com

ipv6 dhcp pool IPV6POOL-A
 dns-server 2001:DB8:ACAD:CAFE::A
 domain-name ccna-lab.com
interface g0/0
 no ip address
 shutdown
 duplex auto
 speed auto
interface g0/1
 no ip address
```

```
duplex auto
speed auto
ipv6 address FE80::1 link-local
ipv6 address 2001:DB8:ACAD:A::11/64
```

```
end
```

Step 5: Load the IPv6 configuration to S1.

```
interface range f0/1-24
  shutdown
```

```
interface range g0/1-2
  shutdown
interface Vlan1
  shutdown
```

```
end
```

Step 6: Save the running configurations on R1 and S1.

Step 7: Verify that IPv6 is enabled on PC-A.

Verify that IPv6 has been enabled in the Local Area Connection Properties window on PC-A.

Part 2: Troubleshoot IPv6 Connectivity

In Part 2, you will test and verify Layer 3 IPv6 connectivity on the network. Continue troubleshooting the network until Layer 3 connectivity has been established on all devices. Do not continue to Part 3 until you have successfully completed Part 2.

Step 4: Troubleshoot IPv6 interfaces on R1.

a. According to the topology, which interface must be active on R1 for network connectivity to be established? Record any commands used to identify which interfaces are active.

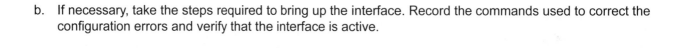

b. If necessary, take the steps required to bring up the interface. Record the commands used to correct the configuration errors and verify that the interface is active.

c. Identify the IPv6 addresses configured on R1. Record the addresses found and the commands used to view the IPv6 addresses.

_____

_____

d. Determine if a configuration error has been made. If any errors are identified, record all the commands used to correct the configuration.

_____

_____

_____

e. On R1, what multicast group is needed for SLAAC to function?

_____

f. What command is used to verify that R1 is a member of that group?

_____

g. If R1 is not a member of the multicast group that is needed for SLAAC to function correctly, make the necessary changes to the configuration so that it joins the group. Record any commands necessary to correct the configurations errors.

_____

```
R1(config)# ipv6 unicast-routing
```

h. Re-issue the command to verify that interface G0/1 has joined the all-routers multicast group (FF02::2).

    Note: If you are unable to join the all-routers multicast group, you may need to save your current configuration and reload the router.

Step 5: Troubleshoot S1.

a. Are the interfaces needed for network connectivity active on S1? _____

    Record any commands that are used to activate necessary interfaces on S1.

_____

_____

_____

_____

b. What command could you use to determine if an IPv6 unicast address has been assigned to S1?

_____

    c.   Does S1 have an IPv6 unicast address configured? If so, what is it?

_____

    d.   If S1 is not receiving a SLAAC address, make the necessary configuration changes to allow it to receive one. Record the commands used.

_____

_____

    e.   Re-issue the command that verifies that the interface now receives a SLAAC address.

    f.   Can S1 ping the IPv6 unicast address assigned to the G0/1 interface assigned to R1?

_____

Step 6: Troubleshoot PC-A.

    a.   Issue the command used on PC-A to verify the IPv6 address assigned. Record the command.

_____

    b.   What is the IPv6 unicast address SLAAC is providing to PC-A?

_____

    c.   Can PC-A ping the default gateway address that was assigned by SLAAC?

_____

    d.   Can PC-A ping the management interface on S1?

_____

_____

_____

    Note: Continue troubleshooting until you can ping R1 and S1 from PC-A.

Part 3: Troubleshoot Stateless DHCPv6

In Part 3, you will test and verify that Stateless DHCPv6 is working correctly on the network. You will need to use the correct IPv6 CLI commands on the router to determine if Stateless DHCPv6 is working. You may want to use debug to help determine if the DHCP server is being solicited.

Step 1: Determine if Stateless DHCPv6 is functioning correctly.

    a.   What is the name of the IPv6 DHCP pool? How did you determine this?

_____

_____

b. What network information is listed in the DHCPv6 pool?

_____

_____

c. Was the DHCPv6 information assigned to PC-A? How did you determine this?

_____

_____

Step 2: Troubleshoot R1.

a. What commands can be used to determine if R1 is configured for Stateless DHCPv6?

_____

_____

b. Is the G0/1 interface on R1 in Stateless DHCPv6 mode?

_____

_____

c. What command can be used to have R1 join the all-DHCPv6 server group?

_____

_____

d. Verify that the all-DHCPv6 server group is configured for interface G0/1.

e. Will PC-A receive the DHCP information now? Explain?

_____

_____

f. What is missing from the configuration of G0/1 that causes hosts to use the DCHP server to retrieve other network information?

_____

g. Reset the IPv6 settings on PC-A.

   1) Open the Local Area Connection Properties window, deselect the Internet Protocol Version 6 (TCP/IPv6) check box, and then click **OK** to accept the change.

   2) Open the Local Area Connection Properties window again, click the Internet Protocol Version 6 (TCP/IPv6) check box, and then click **OK** to accept the change.

h. Issue the command to verify changes have been made on PC-A.

Note: Continue troubleshooting until PC-A receives the additional DHCP information from R1.

Reflection

1. What command is needed in the DHCPv6 pool for Stateful DHCPv6 that is not needed for Stateless DHCPv6? Why?

   _____

   _____

   _____

2. What command is needed on the interface to change the network to use Stateful DHCPv6 instead of Stateless DHCPv6?

   _____

   _____

Router Interface Summary Table

Router Interface Summary				
Router Model	**Ethernet Interface #1**	**Ethernet Interface #2**	**Serial Interface #1**	**Serial Interface #2**
1800	Fast Ethernet 0/0 (F0/0)	Fast Ethernet 0/1 (F0/1)	Serial 0/0/0 (S0/0/0)	Serial 0/0/1 (S0/0/1)
1900	Gigabit Ethernet 0/0 (G0/0)	Gigabit Ethernet 0/1 (G0/1)	Serial 0/0/0 (S0/0/0)	Serial 0/0/1 (S0/0/1)
2801	Fast Ethernet 0/0 (F0/0)	Fast Ethernet 0/1 (F0/1)	Serial 0/1/0 (S0/1/0)	Serial 0/1/1 (S0/1/1)
2811	Fast Ethernet 0/0 (F0/0)	Fast Ethernet 0/1 (F0/1)	Serial 0/0/0 (S0/0/0)	Serial 0/0/1 (S0/0/1)
2900	Gigabit Ethernet 0/0 (G0/0)	Gigabit Ethernet 0/1 (G0/1)	Serial 0/0/0 (S0/0/0)	Serial 0/0/1 (S0/0/1)

Note: To find out how the router is configured, look at the interfaces to identify the type of router and how many interfaces the router has. There is no way to effectively list all the combinations of configurations for each router class. This table includes identifiers for the possible combinations of Ethernet and Serial interfaces in the device. The table does not include any other type of interface, even though a specific router may contain one. An example of this might be an ISDN BRI interface. The string in parenthesis is the legal abbreviation that can be used in Cisco IOS commands to represent the interface.

7.3.1.1 Class Activity – IoE and DHCP

Objective

Configure DHCP for IPv4 or IPv6 on a Cisco 1941 router.

Scenario

This chapter presents the concept of using the DHCP process in a small- to medium-sized business network; however, DHCP also has other uses!

With the advent of the Internet of Everything (IoE), any device in your home capable of wired or wireless connectivity to a network will be able to be accessed from just about anywhere.

Using Packet Tracer for this modeling activity, perform the following tasks:

- Configure a Cisco 1941 router (or DHCP-server-capable ISR device) for IPv4 or IPv6 DHCP addressing.

- Think of five devices in your home you would like to receive IP addresses from the router's DHCP service. Set the end devices to claim DHCP addresses from the DHCP server.

- Show output validating that each end device secures an IP address from the server. Save your output information via a screen capture program or use the **PrtScrn** key command.

- Present your findings to a fellow classmate or to the class.

Required Resources

Packet Tracer software

Reflection

1. Why would a user want to use a Cisco 1941 router to configure DHCP on his home network? Wouldn't a smaller ISR be good enough to use as a DHCP server?

2. How do you think small- medium-sized businesses are able to use DHCP IP address allocation in the IoE and IPv6 network world? Brainstorm and record five possible answers.

Chapter 8 — Wireless LANs

8.0.1.2 Class Activity – Make Mine Wireless

Objective

Explain how wireless LAN components are deployed in a small- to medium-sized business.

Scenario

As the network administrator for your small- to medium-sized business, you realize that your wireless network needs updating, both inside and outside of your building. Therefore, you decide to research how other businesses and educational and community groups set up their WLANs for better access to their employees and clients.

To research this topic, you visit the Customer Case Studies and Research website to see how other businesses use wireless technology. After viewing a few of the videos, or reading some of the case study PDFs, you decide to select two to show to your CEO to support upgrading to a more robust wireless solution for your company.

To complete this class modeling activity, open the accompanying PDF for further instructions on how to proceed.

Resources

Internet access to the WWW

Step 1:   Open your browser and the URL specified for this activity.

a. Choose two case studies about wireless LAN upgrades from the list to read, located on the Customer Case Studies and Research website.

b. As you view the media or read the PDFs, write notes for the following categories:

1) The WLAN *challenge* that the company sought to mitigate

2) The *solution* that was found to the challenge

3) The *results* that were gained by WLAN updates

Step 2:   Share your findings.

a. Share your findings with the class or a classmate.

b. Play the media or show the PDF for one of the case studies you chose from the URL page.

c. In your own words, explain the challenge, solution, and results learned from the media or PDF.

d. Explain how the results you found could be applied to improve your company's network.

8.1.2.10 Lab – Investigating Wireless Implementations

Objectives

Part 1: Explore Integrated Wireless Routers

Part 2: Explore Wireless Access Points

Background / Scenario

The number of mobile devices, such as smart phones, tablets, and laptops, continues to increase. These mobile devices can connect via integrated wireless routers or wireless access points (WAPs) to access the Internet and other network resources. Wireless routers are typically employed in home and small business networks. WAPs are more common in larger, more complex networks.

In this lab, you will explore some integrated wireless routers and Cisco WAPs. You will access online emulators for some of Linksys routers and Cisco WAPs. The emulators imitate the configuration screens for the Linksys routers and Cisco WAPs.

Required Resources

Device with Internet access

Part 1:   Explore Integrated Wireless Routers

Integrated wireless routers usually perform the functions of the following devices:

- a switch by connecting wired devices
- an access point by connecting wireless devices
- a router/gateway by providing access to the Internet through a modem to the ISP

Currently there are many different broadcast standards for wireless routers:

- 802.11b
- 802.11g
- 802.11n
- 802.11ac

The differences between these standards are speed and signal strength. In addition to the standards, each integrated wireless router may have features that meet your network requirement, such as content filtering, QoS, IPv6 support, and wireless security.

In Part 1, you will search the Internet for three different wireless routers and create a list of the important router feature by recording them in the following table. During your search, you can also record additional features that are important to you in the **Other Features** column in the table.

To explore emulators for some of the Linksys routers, go to http://ui.linksys.com/files/.

Note: The Linksys emulators may not provide the most current version of the firmware.

Brand/Model	Price	IPv6-Enabled	Wireless Security	Band	Other Features
Linksys/EA4500	$129.99 USD	Yes	WPA2	Dual-band N (2.4 GHz and 5 GHz)	Separate Guest Network, 4 Gigabit Ethernet Ports, QoS, remote administration from mobile devices, such as smart phones

After you have completed the table above, determine which integrated wireless router you would choose for your home. Explain your choice.

_____

_____

_____

Part 2: Explore Wireless Access Points

Unlike integrated wireless routers, a WAP does not have integrated switch and router functions. A WAP only allows users to access the network wirelessly using mobile devices and provides a connection to the main wired network infrastructure. With the correct user credentials, wireless users can access resources on the network.

In this part, you will explore two Cisco WAPs, WAP321 and AP541N. Cisco's website (http://www.cisco.com) can provide you with technical specifications regarding these WAPs. Furthermore, online emulators are also available at the following links:

To access an online WAP321 emulator, go to http://www.cisco.com/assets/sol/sb/wap321_sps/main.html.

To access an online AP541N emulator, go to https://www.cisco.com/assets/sol/sb/AP541N_GUI/AP541N_1_9_2/Getting_Started.htm.

Model	Security	Band	Other Features / Comments
WAP321			
AP541N			

Reflection

What features on the wireless routers or WAPs are important for your network? Why?

_____

_____

8.4.2.3 Lab – Configuring a Wireless Router and Client

Topology

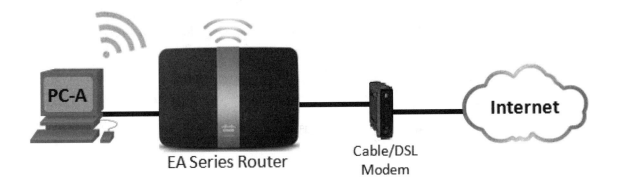

Linksys Router Settings

Network Name (SSID)	CCNA-Net
Network Password	cisconet
Router Password	cisco123

Objectives

Part 1: Configure Basic Settings on a Linksys EA Series Router

Part 2: Secure the Wireless Network

Part 3: Review Additional Features on a Linksys EA Series Router

Part 4: Connect a Wireless Client

Background / Scenario

Surfing the web from anywhere in the home or office has become common. Without wireless connectivity, users would be limited to connect only where there is a wired connection. Users have embraced the flexibility that wireless routers provide for accessing the network and the Internet.

In this lab, you will configure a Linksys Smart Wi-Fi router, which includes applying WPA2 security settings and activating DHCP services. You will review some added features available on these routers, such as USB storage, parental controls, and time restrictions. You will also configure a wireless PC client.

Required Resources

- 1 Linksys EA Series Router (EA4500 with firmware version 2.1.39.145204 or comparable)
- 1 Cable or DSL modem (Optional - needed for Internet service and normally supplied by ISP)
- 1 PC with a Wireless NIC (Windows 7, Vista, or XP)
- Ethernet cables as shown in the topology

Part 1: Configure Basic Settings on a Linksys EA Series Router

The most efficient way to configure basic settings on an EA Series router is to run the Linksys EA Series Setup CD that came with the router. If the Setup CD is unavailable, download the Setup program from http://Linksys.com/support.

Step 1: Insert the Linksys EA-Series Setup CD into the PC.

When prompted, select **Set up your Linksys Router**. You will be asked to read and accept the License Terms for using the software. Click **Next >** after accepting the license terms.

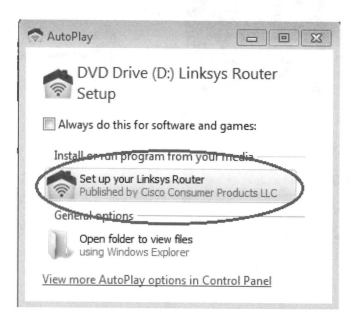

Step 2: Cable the network as shown in the topology.

Follow the directions in the next window for connecting the power cable and Ethernet cable from your cable modem or DSL modem. You may connect the PC to one of the four unused Ethernet ports on the back of the router. After you have connected everything, click **Next >**.

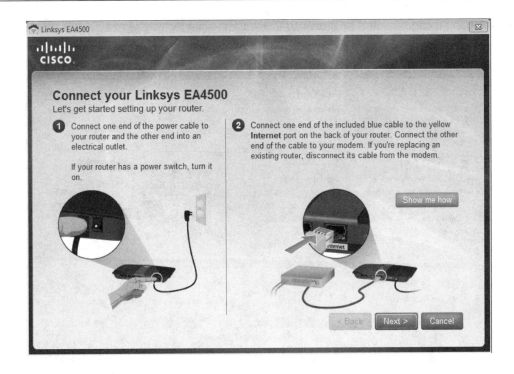

Step 3:   Configure Linksys router settings.

a.   Allow time for the **Linksys router settings** window to display. Use the **Linksys Router Settings** table at the beginning of this lab to fill in the fields in this window. Click **Next** to display the summary router settings screen. Click **Next**.

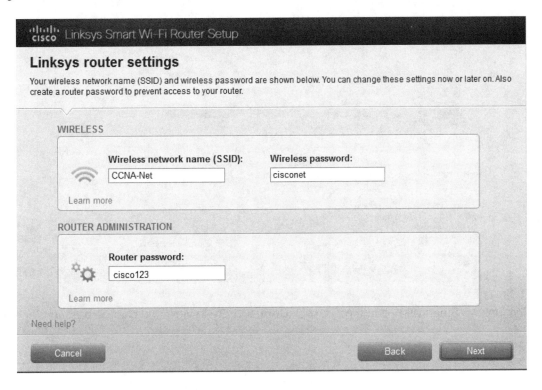

b.   The **Create your Linksys Smart Wi-Fi account** window displays. A Linksys Smart Wi-Fi account associates your router to the account, allowing you to remotely manage the router using a browser or mobile device running the Smart Wi-Fi app. For this lab, bypass the account setup process. Click the **No thanks** box and press **Continue**.

Note: An account can be setup by browsing to www.linksyssmartwifi.com.

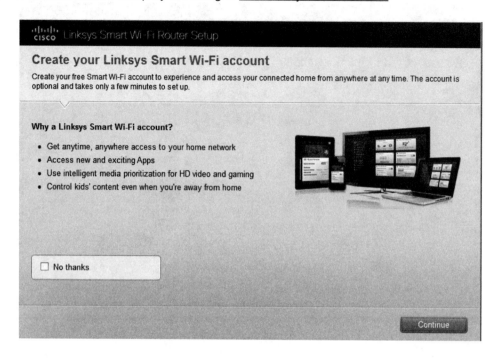

c. A **Sign In** window displays. In the **Access Router** field, enter **cisco123,** and click **Sign In**.

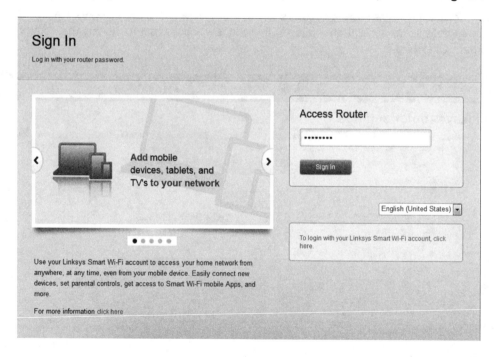

d. On the Linksys Smart Wi-Fi home page, click **Connectivity** to view and change basic router settings.

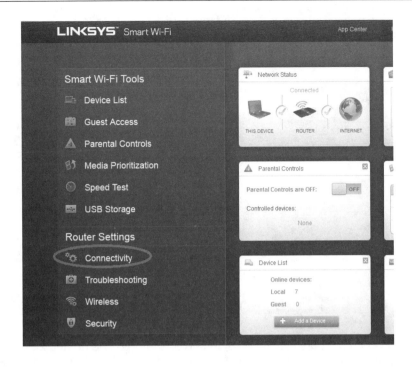

e. On the **Basic** tab, you can edit the SSID name and password, change the router password, perform firm-
    ware updates, and set the time zone for your router. (The router password and SSID information was set
    in Step 3a.) Select the correct time zone for your router from the drop-down box and click **Apply**.

f. The **Internet Settings** tab provides information about the Internet connection. In the example, the router
    automatically configured the connection for DHCP. Both IPv4 and IPv6 information can be displayed from
    this screen.

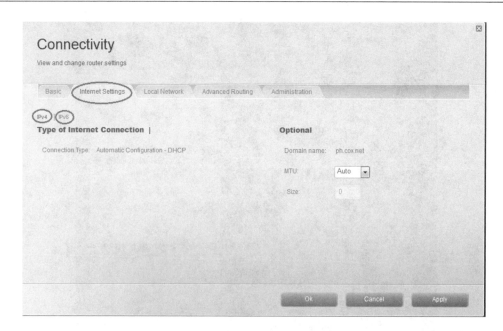

g. The **Local Network** tab controls the local DHCP server settings. The default local network settings specify the 192.168.1.0/24 network and the local IP address of the default router is 192.168.1.1. This can be changed by clicking **Edit** next to **Router Details**. DHCP Server settings can be changed on this screen. You can set the DHCP starting address, maximum number of DHCP users, client lease time, and static DNS servers. Click **Apply** to accept all changes made on this screen.

Note: If DHCP is used to obtain ISP connection information, these DNS addresses will most likely be populated with the ISP's DNS server information.

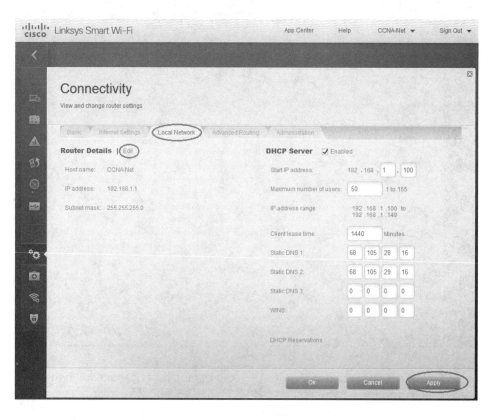

h. The **Advanced Routing** tab allows you to disable Network Address translation (NAT), which is enabled by default. This screen also allows you to add static routes. Click **Apply** to accept any desired changes made on this screen.

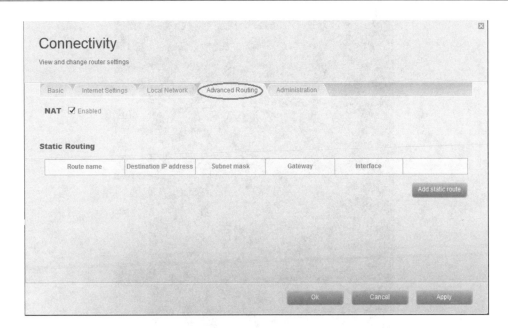

i. The **Administration** tab provides controls for the management of the Smart Wi-Fi software. By chicking the appropriate box, you can activate remote management access to the router. You can also activate HTTPS access and restrict wireless management. Universal Plug and Play (UPnP) and Application Layer Gateway controls are also available on this screen. Click **Apply** to accept any desired changes made on this screen.

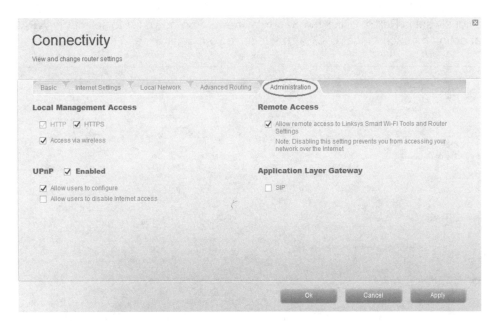

Part 2:   Secure the Wireless Network

In Part 2, you will secure the Linksys EA series router wireless network and review firewall and port forwarding options on a Linksys Smart Wi-Fi router.

Step 1:   Add WPA security on the wireless routers.

a.   From the Linksys Smart Wi-Fi home page, click **Wireless**.

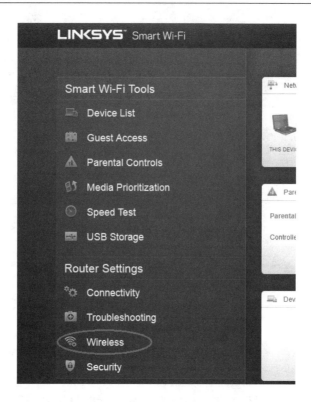

b.   The **Wireless** window displays the settings for both the 2.4 and 5 GHz radios. Use the **Edit** button next to each column to modify the security setting on each wireless frequency range. (The SSID and password were previously set in Part 1.) Click the **Security mode** drop-down list to select the **WPA2/WPA Mixed Personal** option for each range. Click **Apply** to save your settings, and then click **OK**.

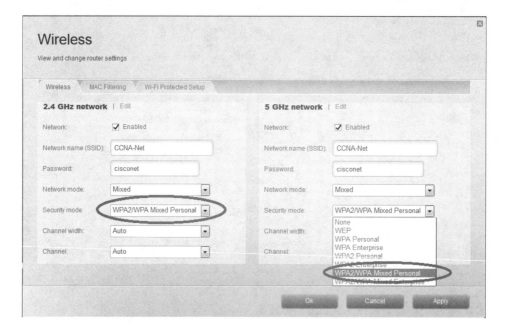

Step 2:   Apply firewall and port forwarding settings.

a.   From the Linksys Smart Wi-Fi home page, click **Security**. In the **Security** windows, the **Firewall**, **DMZ**, and **Apps and Gaming** tabs are available to view and change router security settings.

b. The **Firewall** tab displays firewall settings, where you can enable or disable IPv4 and IPv6 Stateful Packet Inspection (SPI) firewall protection, Virtual Private Network (VPN) Passthrough options, and Internet filters. Click **Apply** to accept any desired changes made on this screen.

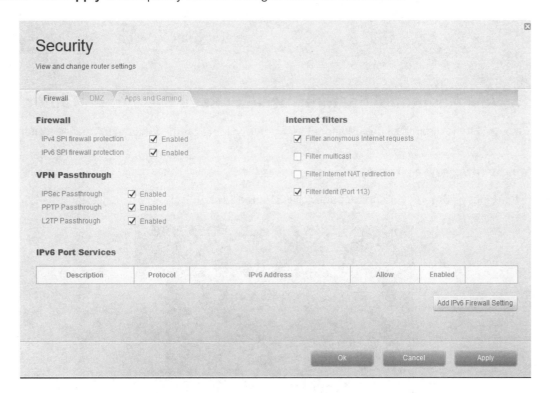

c. The **Apps and Gaming** tab provides port forwarding capabilities. In the example, ports 5060 and 5061 have been opened for a VoIP Softphone application running on a local device at IP address 192.168.1.126. Click **Apply** to accept any desired changes made on this screen.

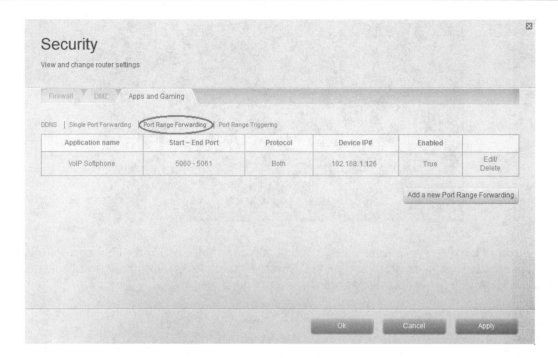

Part 3: Review Additional Features on a Linksys EA Series Router

In Part 3, you will review some of the additional features available on the Linksys EA series router.

Step 1: Review Smart Wi-Fi Tools.

a. From the Linksys Smart Wi-Fi home page, click **Device List**.

The **Device List** window displays the list of clients on the local network. Notice that there is a tab for the **Guest Network**. If the Guest network was activated, clients on that network would be displayed in the **Guest Network** tab.

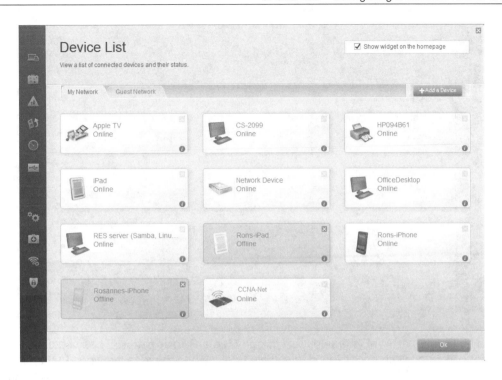

b. From the Linksys Smart Wi-Fi home page, click **Guest Access**. Clients on the guest network only have access to the Internet and are unable to access other clients on the local network. To allow guest access, click on the **Allow guest access** toggle button. Click **Edit** link (next to the Guest network name and password) to change the Guest network password and click **OK** to accept the changes.

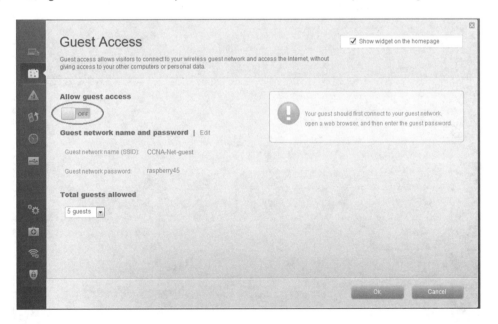

c. From the Linksys Smart Wi-Fi home page, click **Parental Controls**. Use these settings to restrict Internet access on selected devices and to restrict time and websites. Click **OK** to save the settings.

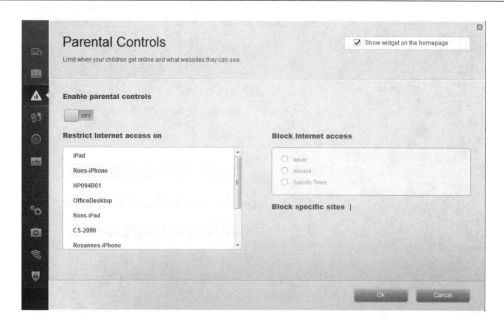

d. From the Linksys Smart Wi-Fi home page, click on **Media Prioritization**. These settings allows you to assign network bandwidth prioritization to selected devices on the local network. In the example, the device labeled Apple TV has been given the highest priority for network resources. To make prioritization changes, just drag and drop the listed devices, and click **OK** to save your settings.

e. From the Linksys Smart Wi-Fi home page, click **Speed Test**. Use this utility to test your Internet access speeds. The example shows the results of the speed test. The router stores the results of each speed tests and allows you to display that history.

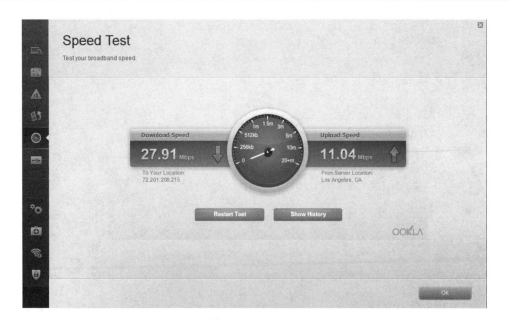

f.   From the Linksys Smart Wi-Fi home page, click **USB Storage**. Use this screen to review your USB drive settings. From here, you can click on the appropriate tab to set up FTP and Media Servers. You can also set up individual user accounts for access to these servers by clicking the tabs at the top of this screen. A USB storage device is plugged into the back of the router to use this option. Click **OK** to save any desired changes.

Step 2: Troubleshoot the router.

From the Linksys Smart Wi-Fi home page, click **Troubleshooting**.

a.   The **Status** tab provides a list of clients on the local network along with their NIC MAC and IP addresses. It also displays how they are connected to the network. Click **OK** to save any desired changes.

b. The **Diagnostics** tab provides the ping and traceroute utilities. It also allows you to reboot the router, backup and restore the router configuration, restore a previous firmware version, release and renew the Internet addresses on your router, and reset to factory default settings. Click **OK** to save any desired changes.

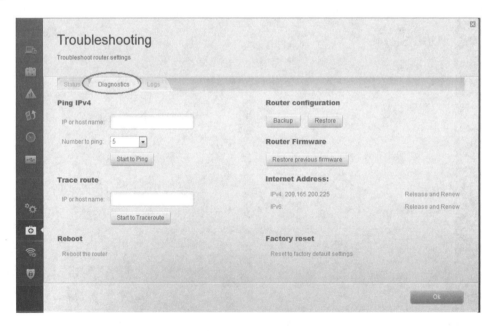

c. The **Logs** tab provides Incoming and Outgoing, Security, and DHCP logs. You can print and clear these logs from this screen. Click **OK** to save any desired changes.

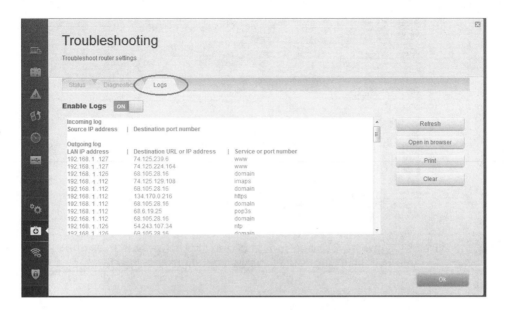

Part 4: Connect a Wireless Client

In Part 4, you will configure the PC's wireless NIC to connect to the Linksys EA Series Router.

Note: This lab was performed using a PC running the Windows 7 operating system. You should be able to perform the lab with other Windows operating systems listed; however, menu selections and screens may vary.

Step 1:   Use the Network and Sharing Center.

a.   Open the **Network and Sharing Center** by clicking the Windows **Start** button > **Control Panel** > **View network status and tasks** under Network and Internet heading in the Category View.

b.   In the left pane, click the **Change adapter settings** link.

The **Network Connections** window provides the list of NICs available on this PC. Look for your **Local Area Connection** and **Wireless Network Connection** adapters in this window.

Note: VPN adapters and other types of network connections may also be displayed in this window.

Step 2:   Work with your wireless NIC.

a.   Select and right-click the **Wireless Network Connection** option to display a drop-down list. If your wireless NIC is disabled, you must **Enable** it.

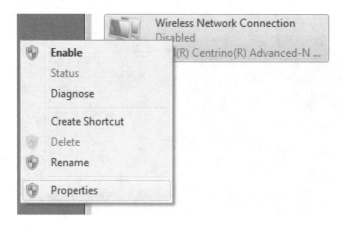

b. Right-click the **Wireless Network Connection**, and then click **Connect/Disconnect**. This displays a list of SSIDs in range of your wireless NIC. Select **CCNA-Net**, then click the **Connect**.

c. When prompted, enter **cisconet** to supply the network security key, and then click **OK**.

d. The wireless icon should display in your taskbar when you have a wireless connection. Click this icon to display the list of SSIDs in range of your PC.

e.   The SSID **CCNA-Ne**t should now show that you are connected to the CCNA-Net wireless network.

Reflection

Why would you not want to use WEP security for your wireless network?

_____

8.5.1.1 Class Activity – Inside and Outside Control

Objective

Explain how wireless LAN components are deployed in a small- to medium-sized business.

Scenario

An assessment has been completed to validate the need for an upgrade to your small- to medium-sized wireless network. Approved for purchase are indoor and outdoor access points and one wireless controller. You must compare equipment models and their specifications before you purchase.

Therefore, you visit the Wireless Compare Products and Services web site and see a features chart for indoor and outdoor wireless access points and controller devices. After reviewing the chart, you note there is some terminology with which you are unfamiliar:

- Federal Information Processing Standard (FIPS)
- MIMO
- Cisco CleanAir Technology
- Cisco FlexConnect
- Band Select

Research the above terms. Prepare your own chart with your company's most important requirements listed for purchasing the indoor and outdoor wireless access points and wireless controller. This chart will assist in validating your purchase order to your accounting manager and CEO.

Resources

Internet access to the World Wide Web

Part 1: Secure Background Knowledge of Wireless Terminology

Step 1: Define unfamiliar wireless terms.
   a. FIPS
   b. MIMO
   c. Cisco CleanAir Technology
   d. Cisco FlexConnect
   e. Band Select

Step 2: Visit the Wireless Compare Products and Services web site.
   a. Compare the devices in each category based on their feature sets.
   b. Choose one model from each category: indoor, outdoor, and controller categories for the upgrades for your business.

Step 3: Create a chart for each device chosen in Step 2b to include:
   a. The main type of selected device (indoor access point, outdoor access point, or controller).
   b. A graphic of each selected device.
   c. Five of the most beneficial features that the selected models would provide your business.

Step 4: After research is complete, explain, and justify your choices with another student, class group, or entire class.